Introduction

This book tells you all about animation, including its historical beginnings, with major emphasis on the here's-how-you-do-it end. It's filled with over 150 photos and illustrations, including some rare photos of animated scenes and early animators, that tell you a visual story on their own.

You'll find information on the detailed techniques you need to create photographic, three-dimensional, computer, slide, and cel animation from the early storyboard stage through the final release print. In addition, plans are included to build your own stand at a fraction of the cost for manufactured stands with similar features. For about $400, you can make a stand that includes a professional Oxberry animation disc with traveling peg bars.

You'll also find useful information on planning and budgeting, and numerous examples on how animation is used in television commercials, public relations films, training and education films, feature films, art and experimental films, and more.

Additional information includes sources for equipment and materials, a helpful glossary of terms, a section on what professional animators in some of the top studios are doing today, and what opportunities there are for you. So read on—and enjoy an educational adventure into The World of Animation.

TABLE OF CONTENTS

PART ONE

A Brief History of Animation

By the Dawn's Early Light

It is difficult to estimate the tremendous amount of time and energy that goes into the millions of cels drawn to fill a comparatively small amount of film footage. If a young artist starting today were to look at his time at the drawing board, and that alone, he would probably not start. But that isn't what the animation pioneers looked at in the early days. They were in love with something so new, so magic, and so promising that the hours, months, and years slipped by very quickly.

One such pioneer was the late Max Fleischer, whose career was summarized in the Milestones column of TIME Magazine for September 25, 1972. The column read:

> "DIED: Max Fleischer, 89, dean of movie cartoonists, who in the '20's and '30's brought to the screen Popeye the Sailor, Betty Boop, and the "Out of the Inkwell" cartoon series; in Los Angeles. Fleischer's first animated feature, made in 1917, took a year to create and ran less than one minute . . ."

Although we've lost a giant among animation artists, Max Fleischer's contributions live on in his films. During the two decades that followed the release of his first animated feature, he acquired over two dozen patents for the innovative production techniques that made his style so special. Leslie Carbarga's book THE FLEISCHER STORY (published by Crown Publishers of New York in 1976) is probably the first in a long series of books that reflect a continuing interest in the visual creativity of this fine artist.

But the history of animation began long before Max Fleischer picked up his pen to create . . . it started over 30,000 years ago in the caves of France and Spain, where Neanderthals drew running and vaulting animals, with multiple limbs, to suggest "living" motion. We can see samples of more sophisticated efforts in pre-Christian Egyptian, Greek, and Roman times when warriors used to spin their circular shields at campfires to show a series of silhouettes, painted in sequence on the outside of their shields, that appeared to be in motion.

It must have been this challenge of creating "motion" that captivated the Dutch scientist Pieter van Musschenbroek, who created the first animated image using a forerunner of the modern slide projector in 1736. This device was developed almost a century earlier by two Jesuit priests, Althanasius Kircher and Gaspar Schott, and originally featured a straight row of slides. Later Schott modified the design to create a rotary slide disc which Musschenbroek found intriguing. Musschenbroek used this instrument to project a series of slides, each depicting a hand-drawn image of a windmill with slight variations in position, to create the illusion of motion. The "magic lantern," as the projector was called, enjoyed wide popularity for some time until it was lost to history and the ongoing fascination with newer mechanical devices that more effectively produced moving images.

About a century after Musschenbroek's animated windmill, Peter Mark Roget made a substantial contribution to the development of motion pictures, as well as the

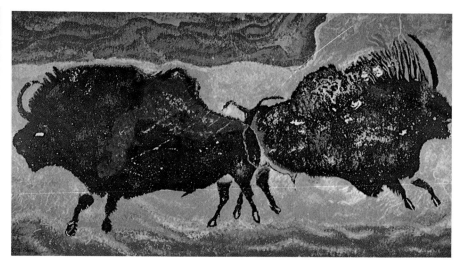

Two stampeding bison on an 8-foot long panel. Lascaux, France. 18,000 years B.C.

Bull with six legs and two tails—extra limbs and tail have been added to create an impression of movement. Eastern Spanish rock painting. 8,000 years B.C. (Silk screens by D. Mazonowicz, Gallery of Prehistoric Art, NYC)

art of animation by publishing what is now considered a classic work: PERSISTENCE OF VISION WITH REGARD TO MOVING OBJECTS.* This 1824 study established four basic principles: "The viewer's vision must be restricted to one still picture at a time; the eye blurs many images into one image if they are presented in quick succession; a certain minimum speed is required to produce this blurring effect; and finally, a large quantity of light is essential to create a convincing image." The very same year that Roget published his study, Joseph Nicephore Niepce, an inventor and lithographer living in central France, produced the first true photograph. Both events provided a vital stimulus towards the development of motion pictures and the art of film animation. Roget's study influenced Joseph Plateau, a Belgian artist-scientist, who developed the phenakistoscope in 1829 based on the "Persistence of Vision" principles. Plateau's invention had a series of sixteen pictures mounted on a spinning disc. As the disc was spun, the viewer looked through an opening that restricted the

*Roget's study has been refuted in a paper by Joseph Anderson and Barbara Fisher, published in volume 30, number 4 in the Fall issue of the Journal of the University Film Association. But, despite this fact, it still played a significant role in the development of motion pictures.

view to one image at a time, as Roget's theory suggested. Thus, the illusion of motion was created. In a short time, the major cities of the world offered over a hundred variations of this new "toy" with "moving" pictures of running dogs, horses, monkeys,

The phenomenon of the zoetrope and other toys that utilized an image in "motion" was the platform from which the early newspaper cartoonists would later launch their animation concepts. (Courtesy of the International Museum of Photography at the George Eastman House)

Typical of the zoetrope and other devices was a vaulting figure such as this one from a late nineteenth century device. Subjects were often taken from circus life. (Courtesy of the International Museum of Photography at the George Eastman House)

fish, and acrobats. They were called a variety of names from the animatoscope to zoetrope. The commercial popularity of this technical development interested entrepreneurs, and soon Emile Renaud opened the first parlour theatre in Paris to show hand-drawn "moving" pictures synchronized with music. The phenakistoscope and the interest it aroused set the stage for the dramatic developments in the last decade of the 19th Century: the invention of the camera by the Edison Company, the invention of film by Eastman Kodak Company, and the first successful film projection by the Lumière brothers in 1896. These inventions, combining principles that dated back before the development of the "magic lantern" and those discovered much later, not only helped to refine and expand the art of animation, but also set its special potential before the world.

George Eastman's film and Thomas Edison's camera. Although several others were working on the concept of motion pictures, such as the Lumiere brothers in France, it was these two pioneers who made it a feasible commercial concept.

Joseph Pulitzer and His Yellow Kid—The Emergence of the New York City Animators

About the same time the inventions of Edison, Eastman, and the Lumière brothers were introduced, something very exciting was happening in the newspaper industry that would have a great impact on the development of animation. To adequately understand and appreciate the circumstances, let's step back a few years to New York City in 1883. That was the year Joseph Pulitzer left St. Louis and came east to a booming New York City. Once there, he bought the declining NEW YORK WORLD and virtually turned it upside down, giving it a new flair and style born of ambition. Pulitzer was then 36 years old.

With the coming of Joseph Pulitzer and his powerful drive in New York, the competition for newsstand sales really began. William Randolph Hearst, another newcomer to New York, bought the JOURNAL, started to imitate Pulitzer, and was clearly out to top the man from St. Louis.

While the wild headlines on both newspapers churned up circulation, Pulitzer sought an additional "edge." In 1893, he bought a Hoe four-color rotary press to print famous works of art for his NEW YORK WORLD'S Sunday supplement. The effort did not meet with success, but Pulitzer's Sunday editor Morrill Goddard talked him into using the equipment for comic art similar to the work done in JUDGE, PUCK, and LIFE, the most popular humor magazines of the time. Goddard hired Richard Outcalt, a young American comic artist, who created the first comic series, DOWN IN HOGAN'S ALLEY, published in 1895. HOGAN'S ALLEY, as the series came to be called, attempted to burlesque current events using a group of neighborhood ragamuffins. The setting was the city slums—squalid tenements and backyards filled with dogs, cats, and little tough guys. One of the street urchins was a nameless, flap-eared, one-toothed, bald-headed kid dressed in a long, dirty nightshirt, the front of which was often used for additional commentary.

At this time most of the problems associated with color printing had been solved, but yellow ink still had a tendency to smudge on newsprint. Charles Saalberg, foreman of the color press at the WORLD, decided to experiment with a quick-drying tallow-yellow ink. He turned to Outcalt's HOGAN'S ALLEY and arbitrarily chose the bald-headed urchin's nightshirt for a test area. The following Sunday, a splash of pure, bright yellow attracted every eye to Outcalt's cartoon. The YELLOW KID was born and with him the comic strip.

The close association of wild headlines with this new yellow-shirted comic strip character in the same paper gave rise to a name for the type of journalism in vogue at that time. Thus, the sensational headlines with stories that were more fiction than fact became known as "yellow journalism."

It was Richard Outcalt and the comic strip artists following him

It was 1895 "Down in Hogan's Alley," and amidst the tattered kids in backyard tenement slums was a cartoon waif in a yellow nightshirt. From this amusing and fine cartoon expression came comic strip art, the name "yellow journalism" and later, the animated cartoon.

THE AMATEUR DIME MUSEUM IN HOGAN'S ALLEY.

who gave birth to animated art on film. Virtually all of the early animators started as comic strip artists. In those early days they were pirated, traded, and sold off for great amounts of money, much as ballplayers are today. In a laughable battle between Pulitzer and Hearst, the latter hired away the former's entire cartoon staff for his paper. The staff was then hired back by Pulitzer and, finally hired by Hearst again for his JOURNAL. In the end, the staff remained with Hearst while an angry, frustrated Pulitzer developed a new staff.

Among the more famous comic strip artists was the brilliant Winsor McCay at the Cincinnati COMMERCIAL TRIBUNE in 1897, John R. Bray at the Detroit EVENING NEWS in 1900, and Max Fleischer, whom Bray joined at the Brooklyn DAILY EAGLE in 1901.

Yet another was James Stewart Blackton, a cartoonist and reporter for the New York EVENING WORLD. Some historians credit French animator Emile Cohl with the first animated film, but American animator-historian John Canemaker credits Blackton with the first two animated films: THE ENCHANTED DRAWING in 1900 and HUMOROUS PHASES OF FUNNY FACES in 1906. Although Cohl did give us the first animated series called PHANTASMAGORIE and the first animated character star named Fantouche, he used a simple blackboard technique (white lines on black background) with stick figures.

Following both earlier pioneers was a man they both influenced— Winsor McCay—who put his news-paper-born LITTLE NEMO on film in 1911. He gave us the first fluid animation, unlike the earlier pioneer's jerky motion. In the beginning, McCay drew on translu-cent rice paper using crude cross-marks for registration from one frame to another, but even his early work, which can be seen today in cinema museums, is amazingly smooth. John A. Fitzsimmons in an unpublished paper, "My Days with Winsor McCay," tells:

> "After each drawing was completed and a serial number assigned to it, marks for keeping it in register with the other drawings were placed on the upper right and left corners. To facilitate handling and the photographing of the drawings, mounting them on slightly larger pieces of light cardboard became the next step. The left side and bottom of these mounts were cut at an absolute ninety-degree angle, and the register marks printed on them had to correspond exactly with the location of the register marks on the tissue drawings, which had marks to be placed precisely over those on the cardboard. The purpose of being so critical regarding this phase of the operation was the urgency of eliminating all unnecessary vibration of the picture on the screen."

Later, Fitzsimmons developed a cel registration system for McCay that was the forerunner of most peg systems used today.

McCay also introduced animation cycles (the repeated use of a series of cels to show a particular movement), a technique frequently used in today's

Winsor McCay's LITTLE NEMO newspaper comic strip was animated on motion picture film in 1911.
(© Nostalgia Press, Inc.)

children's cartoon productions to save the artist time and effort. He used this cycle technique in his second film, HOW A MOSQUITO OPERATES, and extensively in his highly successful film, GERTIE, THE TRAINED DINOSAUR.

Progress in the field of animation continued, and in 1913 Raoul Barre established the first studio capable of producing animated cartoons in quantity. The same year, John Bray (a newspaper comic strip artist mentioned earlier) developed the first studio-produced animated series: COLONEL HEESA LIAR IN AFRICA. Earlier that year Bray released THE ARTIST'S DREAM, also known as THE DACHSHUND AND THE SAUSAGE.

With the advent of commercialized animation, came the need for animators to protect their special techniques with patents. Probably the most significant patent issued to an early animator was filed in December 1914 and granted in June 1915. It involved the cel animation process, in which art was placed on a transparent piece of celluloid over common backgrounds. The man granted the patent was Earl Hurd of Kansas City. The same year, Max Fleischer, who was then art editor at POPULAR SCIENCE, filed for a patent in 1917 for a device that allowed the animator to trace over live-action images to assure life-like smooth animation called the rotoscope.

In 1917, John Bray wisely combined his talents and resources with Earl Hurd. Together, they owned most of the new animation patents and collected large royalties from all the other animators of the period. They continued to do so until the patents ran out seventeen years later.

© King Features Syndicate.

Felix the Cat, probably the most famous of the early cartoon characters, was created by Otto Mesmer at the Pat Sullivan Studio in New York. (© Felix the Cat Productions, Inc.)

As the techniques proliferated and new animators appeared, the stage was set for the development of a cartoon star—a character with "personality" that would develop a large audience following. The task was accomplished by Otto Messmer in the Pat Sullivan studio when he created Felix the Cat.

Felix the Cat was the hottest cartoon property around during the '20s, and his clever antics often paralleled the great comic talents of Chaplin and Keaton. But 1927 brought two things: sound on film and the loss of Felix.

Wonderful Felix, who walked and ran to the click of sprocket holes, piano music, or whatever the theatre musicians happened to be playing, had a short-lived career. Pat Sullivan, who owned him, refused to believe that Felix needed sound accompaniment. But before Felix passed into history, he helped give impetus to the new golden age of animation. Felix ushered in the greatest genius in the artform to date: Walt Disney.

The Kid from Kansas City: The Disney Era

Walt Disney was born in Kansas City in 1901, at almost the same time Blackton's first cartoon film, THE ENCHANTED DRAWING, was released. By the time he went west to California at age 21, he had already headed up his own studio back in Kansas City. All of Disney's early films were greatly influenced by the prevailing animation styles of the 1900-to-1920 period. There were little mice that looked suspiciously like those from Paul Terry's FARMER AL FALFA series. Disney's Oswald the Lucky Rabbit and even the early Mickey Mouse appeared to be related to Felix the Cat. Indeed, Disney's ALICE'S WONDER-LAND, which brought him his first distribution contract, was a mixture of live action and anima-tion much like Max Fleischer's earlier and on-going OUT OF THE INKWELL series. This was a time of smiling animals designed for ease of handling in the time-consuming animation process. The financial rewards were sometimes meager, but the mere joy of the creative pursuit seemed to be enough for some.

From those early beginnings, Disney's true talent came to the fore as both creative director of the studio and inspiration to the many artists looking for work. Walt Disney was not born to play solo, but to orchestrate a major step forward in the history of animation. He created a new standard of achievement to which others would aim. One of his greatest accomplishments occurred following an upsetting legal defeat. In 1927, Disney lost legal control of his OSWALD THE LUCKY RABBIT, perhaps the finest animated character of that time. Margaret Winkler, his New York distributor, won the rights to Oswald on the ground that her husband, Charles Mintz, named the rabbit. Winkler wanted more profit from the already profitable Oswald films and hired away much of the Disney staff to produce the films without Disney. This marked the end for Oswald, but it opened the way for the great new Mickey Mouse.

In a radio interview several years before his death (in 1966), Disney noted that his wife Lillian named Mickey on the train back from the Winkler meeting in New York. His choice was Mortimer, the name of a pet mouse he once had back in Kansas City. But Lillian contended that Mortimer didn't have the right "bounce." Disney agreed, and Mickey Mouse was born.

As "legend" has it, Walt Disney's early mouse (left) was called Mortimer. Credit for the lively name of Mickey goes to Walt's wife, Lillian. The rounded Mickey on the right was designed by Ub Iwerks, who animated many of the early Mickey Mouse shorts. (© Walt Disney Productions)

Ubbe "Ub" Iwerks (pronounced "eye works") (on the right) was Disney's chief animator in the early days; Iwerks also contributed many technical innovations to the studio over the long span of his tenure. (© Walt Disney Productions)

It was Ubbe "Ub" Iwerks who refined Mickey into a fast-drawn happy mouse that was easy to work with on cels. He was a fine engineer and superb animator who consistently reshaped and refined the animation process, coming up with many new techniques and more flexible equipment that contributed immeasurably to Disney's success.

Ub Iwerks and Walt Disney were so excited about the new character, Mickey Mouse, that they planned two cartoons immediately. The first, PLANE CRAZY, was finished in 1927 and the second, GALLOPIN' GAUCHO, was on the drawing boards and scripted when a very dramatic event occurred.

On Sunday, October 23, 1927, Warner Brothers released THE JAZZ SINGER, a live-action film with synchronized sound played on a sound projection system called a Vitaphone. The effect created was that the characters appeared to talk and sing on screen! Pictures actually talked and the audiences loved it! Max Fleischer had previously used unsynchronized sound in cartoons, and a few others had experimented with background sound effects, but none of these attempts made the impact that the synchronized sound in THE JAZZ SINGER did.

Disney, who characteristically was willing to take a chance on new ventures, realized the potential

that synchronized sound offered. He decided not to release PLANE CRAZY, and he also held up completion of GALLOPIN' GAUCHO to move in a new direction. He chose to plan a sound track first and then animate to the beat of the music. Rather than relying on spoken jokes for his effects, Disney kept the traditional emphasis on action and supported it with carefully timed sound effects and a strongly rhythmical music sound track. This first sound cartoon venture, which also introduced Mickey Mouse to the public, was STEAMBOAT WILLIE, released more than a half century ago, in 1928. In the film, Mickey and Minnie Mouse transform the cargo of a riverboat, including livestock, into an orchestra. The effect was astounding and Mickey was securely launched in grand Hollywood style. Walt Disney was only 26 when STEAMBOAT WILLIE was released, and four years later he received an Academy Award for creating Mickey Mouse.

That same year in 1932, Disney introduced yet another film innovation. His film FLOWERS AND TREES, a forerunner of FANTASIA, was released in full color. From that release on, color was used for nearly all animated cartoons.

The Disney contributions in the art of animation are too numerous to list here. Their importance to the field of film animation can be gauged by the 1,461 awards the Disney Studio has received from various organizations throughout the world.

The Modern Short- and Medium-Length Theatrical Film

There were other studios who, along with Disney in the thirties and forties, created theatrical short films that have been popular for the last four decades. The Warner Brothers studio included the talents of Hugh Harman, Rudolph Ising, and Isadore "Friz" Freleng from the old Schlesinger studio who joined Warner Brothers in the early 30s. This group created the memorable LOONEY TUNES series. Later, other fine animators joined this studio, including Tex Avery, Bob Clampett, Bob McKimson and Chuck Jones, who worked on the popular series called MERRY MELODIES. Unlike Disney's penchant for action and sight-gags, the Warner's studio relied on verbal cleverness and slapstick humor which were verboten at the Disney studio. So powerful and well-known are the characters they created that the mere mention of Bugs Bunny, Porky Pig, Daffy Duck, or the Roadrunner still brings smiles to faces in any audience.

Along with the Warner's studio, Universal had a cartoon division headed by Walter Lantz, who created WOODY WOODPECKER, and at Columbia's Screen Gems, Ben Harrison and Manny Gould created the SCRAPPY and KRAZY KAT series. Paramount distributed Max Fleischer's POPEYE THE SAILOR, and the TERRY TOONS cartoons, created by Paul Terry, were distributed by 20th Century Fox. The MGM studio also contributed with the popular Bill Hanna and Joe Barbera series, TOM AND JERRY, which has since become a classic.

In 1950, a new type of cartoon was introduced by United Productions of America. The UPA group, made up mostly of former Disney artists who wanted a new approach to animation, came up with characters such as Gerald McBoing Boing and Mr. Magoo. These cartoons were considered a fresh departure from the Disney style and employed the first intentional use of limited motion (animation of only one part of the body) by American artists, along with highly stylized line art. The popularity of limited motion continues today, as evidenced by most of the cartoons currently produced for television.

These three Warner Brothers' stars brought new concepts and expression to the famous animation studio, thanks to the creative genius of animators like Isadore "Friz" Freleng, Bob Clampett, and Tex Avery. For those who haven't been introduced— (from left to right) Bugs Bunny, Porky Pig, and Daffy Duck.

Produced by Max Fleischer and directed by Dave Fleischer, the 1939 feature length release, GULLIVER'S TRAVELS, after the Jonathan Swift satire, was perhaps the Fleischer studios' greatest achievement. It had brilliant inventiveness and superbly animated characters. (Feature distributed by National Telefilm Association, Inc., Los Angeles, who authorized use of photographs.)

The Animated Feature Film

There were a number of partially animated features that preceded Walt Disney's first full-length feature, SNOW WHITE AND THE SEVEN DWARFS, released in 1938. The first of these, made in Italy by Giovanni Pastrone and entitled THE WAR AND THE DREAM OF MOMI, combined puppets and live action and was released and distributed by Itala-Film in 1916. Another, also Italian, was Raoul Verdini's THE ADVENTURES OF PINOCCHIO which was released in 1936, four years prior to the Disney version of the Carlo Collodi classic. In 1935, Russia produced a puppet and live-action film, THE NEW GULLIVER, followed by another similar production in 1939, THE LITTLE GOLDEN KEY, both by Alexander Ptuschko.

The two fully animated films produced before SNOW WHITE were of a very different subject matter. One, lost in a fire in 1969, was a political satire by Frederico Valle entitled THE APOSTLE, released in 1917. The other, also a political satire, was directed, written, and produced by one of the assistant directors of THE APOSTLE, Quirino Cristiani, and was entitled PELUDO-POLIS, released in 1931. This latter film used both the Vita-phone system and color.

The Disney studio dominated the early years of feature animation, releasing a long string of films after SNOW WHITE. Other distinguished efforts in the same time period included the Fleischer brothers' GULLIVER'S TRAVELS and MR. BUG GOES TO TOWN, and the first Russian animated art film, THE HUNCH-BACKED HORSE. But the production of full-length animated

Mr. Bug and Honeybee go steppin'. The Fleischer brothers' second animated feature, MR. BUG (HOPPITY) GOES TO TOWN, was a breakthrough in original story concept and one of the finest examples of animation of all time. Unfortunately, the film was never promoted properly and is just being recognized today, almost four decades after its release. (Feature distributed by National Telefilm Association, Inc., Los Angeles, who authorized use of photographs.)

feature films really didn't get underway until the 1950s. Since then, the world has seen such animators as Czechoslovakia's Jiri Trnka, who developed puppet animation to a high art, and England's John Halas and Joy Batchelor, producers of the controversial ANIMAL FARM in 1954. Also from England is George Dunning, producer of THE YELLOW SUBMARINE (1968), a film filled with cartoons and pixilation that was a fresh departure from the traditional style. This need for a departure from tradition continues into the seventies with fresh new talents who are as anxious as the early pioneers of animation to begin something novel and exciting. A good example is Ralph Bakshi (United States) who produced FRITZ THE CAT (1972) and HEAVY TRAFFIC (1973) for adult audiences, and the more recent LORD OF THE RINGS (1978), for children and adults. Bakshi's latest, LORD OF THE RINGS, was created using several animation techniques, including rotoscoping. For this technique, live action is filmed first, and then every other frame is traced to create an animated scene. This technique allowed Bakshi to depict motion accurately and animate scenes with six or more moving figures. He also used cel animation, as well as live-action footage that was painted with a colored wash.

Enthusiasm for animation continues to increase on the part of the animators and the audiences they create for. World production to date is estimated at more than 200 feature films, and the growing interest in both traditional and contemporary applications is a good indication of its strong future. As new innovations in the art continue, and seemingly endless creative possibilities are sought, the development of animation continues in the same spirit it was created. Remember, it was Winsor McCay, Max Fleischer, Walt Disney, and all the other greats who taught us that nothing was really impossible. It only seemed that way.

PART TWO

The Mechanics of Animation

Introduction

There is more to the mechanics of producing an animated sequence than choosing and developing the animation technique you want to use. Whether you choose the technique of photographic, cel, three-dimensional, slide, or computer animation, the same planning stage is necessary to develop the idea you want to communicate, put it in story form, and create a sound track to accompany it—all before the actual animation production process begins. So we've included a few basics for you to consider on developing a story and creating a sound track, followed by a more in-depth description of the basic animation techniques you can use in your production.

Developing the Story

Once you have an idea for a film, the next step is to develop the idea into a story that effectively communicates what you want to say. Whether your idea is to promote a product or service, communicate a personal philosophy, create a fairytale, or teach a special technique—everything must have a beginning and an end.

Once you decide where your story will begin, make a good story commitment by developing it in a logical progression. The best way to do this is by "storyboarding" your line of thought on small index cards that indicate your direction. Start out by writing down your beginning and drawing a picture to visualize what you want to show. Then, continue to develop your story on each succeeding card, until you reach the end.

The next step is to line up your cards in front of you, in the order you've chosen, to see if there's a logical progression of thought from beginning to end. If not, do some reworking and juggle around the order of your cards until you're satisfied. Once you've established your story line and rough visuals, the scripting that follows is a matter of expanding and detailing the ideas on your cards into a finished story that you can work from. A good way to do this is in a two-column format, with the left column indicating the visual and information on camera motion (zooms, pans, etc) and the right column indicating dialogue and other sound track information.

The Sound Track and Its Importance

Before we begin to discuss the "how-to's" for the basic animation techniques, let's first talk about the importance of a sound track. A good sound track is an essential element that can make or break a film. Moreover, in animation, the art should be an extension of the sound track. Because many animators believe this, the sound track is considered a top-priority item in the animation industry. In films that have synchronized voice and character lip movements or art that is supportive of the sound, such as in the case of photoanimation, the sound should always be recorded first. In cases where the film has background music or a "voice-over" narration, the sound can be done at a later point.

The process of building a sound track involves recording the narrative or dialogue and music that your script indicates on separate tracks that will later be synchronized and mixed together. Profes-

sional animation studios usually record sound on perforated magnetic film. But if you don't have the equipment needed to do this, you can first record on quarter-inch magnetic tape and then have a commercial sound studio transfer the sound to magnetic film, which should be 16 mm or 35 mm.

Ideally, the initial tape recording should be done on a machine equipped with a synchronous pulse, which helps to ensure that the sound will be recorded at a fixed rate equivalent to the speed of the camera. Many professional tape recorders have the synchronous pulse device; if yours does not, it can probably be adapted by a sound engineering firm that specializes in the construction of custom recorders and sound systems.

When the recording is complete, the separate tracks of dialogue, music, etc, on magnetic film are put on a synchronizer, to create a frame-by-frame registration or synchronization between the

The synchronizer (left of the right-hand rewind reel), along with the other standard editing equipment shown on this editing table, is used to put two or more films in synchronization.

sound tracks. The synchronizer is a ganged series of sprockets, with a sound head on the top of each one. When the separate tracks of magnetic film are placed on the individual sprockets, the sounds on the film are "read" by the sound head as the film passes under it. The sound head, similar to that found on a tape recorder, is connected to a sound reader that amplifies any sound on the tracks. The use of this synchronizer makes it possible to precisely measure the number of frames in each word, syllable, and musical beat as well as the number of frames in the pauses between words and sentences. When these syllables, beats, etc, are heard on the sound reader, they can be marked on the film with a white, grease or china marker pencil to indicate the desired accents or lip movements on a frame-by-frame basis. This information can then be written on a bar sheet, on which each space corresponds to a frame on the magnetic film. The bar sheet provides a visual record of dialogue and music. In situations where the sound is done first, this bar sheet will be used as a work sheet to plan animation that matches the dialogue and music on the sound track.

When the bar sheet is filled out, remember that it's not necessary to make a record of each vowel or consonant for plotting lip-sync (mouth action) animation, since the purpose of lip animation is not to imitate the realistic movements of living persons, but to present those movements in a representative manner that will be acceptable to the viewer. Extreme accuracy in simulating lip movements usually results in overarticulation that appears forced and unnatural; in real life most people are lip-lazy. A simple visual pattern in which the open lips generally match the open vowels is usually sufficient.
For some animators, the accents of speech are consonants because they call for closed lip movements. They think that perfect synchronization of words comprising letters such as b, m, and p gives credibility to the line of dialogue, rendering it acceptable, even if the remainder of the sentence is only vaguely patterned. However, other animators prefer to use vowels such as o and e for opened lip movements.

Plotting is not as critical for animation that is merely to parallel narration or music. It is sufficient to have a beginning, accent or emphasis spots, and an ending plotted for synchronization with the track. An exception to this is animation that is coupled to a musical rhythm, using a beat method to plot the action. After the sound tracks are put in sync with each other and the bar sheets are filled out, the tracks are set aside until the animation is completed. Then a final mix is made, combining the tracks, which will eventually be matched with the final animation footage. It is at this point, when the visual is complete, that sound effects are often added. Additional information on sound will be covered in the following section on basic animation techniques. Also, for more in-depth information on sound, refer to Kodak's publication, SOUND: MAGNETIC SOUND RECORDING FOR MOTION PICTURES (S-75).

Animation film editor Maxwell Seligman plots bar sheets from pure sound beats. The color-coded bar graphs indicate not only beat-to-frame position, but music peaks and type of instruments, as well as tempo changes.

Basic Animation Techniques

Photographic Animation

Visualize the opening scene in Walt Disney's PINOCCHIO. It begins with a panoramic view of an Alpine village. As the scene opens, the camera moves down from the moon and the mountaintops to a little Alpine village, past the church steeple, the moonlit chimneys, and finally down a cobblestone street to Geppetto's candle-lit workshop. This entire scene was photographed in a steady, flowing movement,

The opening scene for Walt Disney's Pinocchio is a brilliant example of how photographic animation helps a motion picture. In it, we soar silently and effortlessly from the night sky, past the church steeple and chimneys, down to the cobblestone street and Geppetto's Workshop.
(© Walt Disney Productions)

without cuts, across a single piece of magnificent artwork. The illusion it creates, much like the first scene in Disney's PETER PAN, is of a scene you might see from a helicopter flying above a village. This technique is called photographic animation, or photoanimation. The essential aspect of this type of animation is that art or photographic stills are filmed with a camera in motion, the animation stand compound in motion, or a combination of both.

Some filmmakers don't consider this type of filming true animation. But to animate literally means "to give life to." When stills are used, there are many creative possibilities open to you. You can film photographs from any historical period and mix them with art from the same period or any period that makes an imaginative combination with the photographs. For example, a film on the American Civil War could be made using classic photos taken during that period, combined with realistic or stylized art to make the visuals come alive.

The science of photographic animation has been developed to such a point that Comcorps, a company in Washington, D.C., has made entire films from 35 mm slides of human organs. Comcorps has developed an aerial-image device that projects an optical image of a 35 mm slide wide enough to pan across for ten seconds at a fairly fast pace, without stopping. If given a slide with a great deal of information on it, such as a picture of Brueghel's CHILDREN'S GAMES, they can make an entire short film from a single 35 mm slide by panning, zooming, and cutting from one part of the art to another to illustrate a narrative. This aerial-image process has the ability to go through another generation of film with minimal build-up of contrast or deterioration of image quality.

All films that utilize the photographic animation process are produced using the same general technique. The first step is usually to produce the sound track. Narration is completed, or dialogue between two or more performers, or a combination of both. Music is added to the spoken word or the narrative track to heighten the dramatic effect and enhance the mood you are trying to create. These elements—narrative and music—are recorded on 16 mm or 35 mm magnetic film. Sometimes the music and dialogue are mixed at the recording stage, but when there are two or more separate tracks, a synchronizer is used to match the tracks and the sound information is plotted on a bar sheet, as mentioned in the earlier section on sound. This bar sheet is also used for any other form of

animation, including full-motion or "classic" animation. As we can see in the example, it is divided into frame and running foot segments, providing the animator with a visual guide to the sound track.

The next step involves selecting the visuals to be filmed on the animation stand and planning the movements of the camera (on a vertical plane) and the animation stand compound (on a horizontal plane). The bar sheet for the sound track is then used, along with the art, to plot exposure sheets that the animation stand operator will use as a guide for filming. The bar sheet information is used to synchronize the sound with the camera moves. When art

ComCorps cameraman programs the "Film-O-Graphic™" camera for the aerial image filming of transparencies of any size. Image information from slides can be transferred to any film format from 16mm through 70mm introducing special-effects factors to bring a new dimension of image transmission to filmmakers. (© ComCorps)

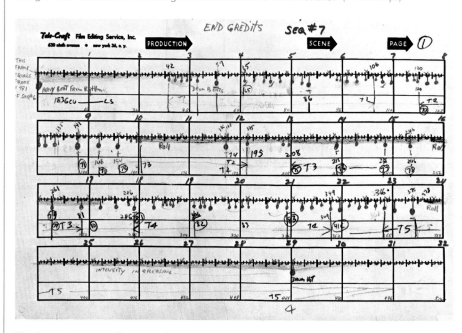

The bar sheet contains sound track elements that are broken down to single frames. It is one of the most important steps prior to the development of the exposure sheet.

is plotted into exposure sheets, the field size (the area the camera sees on the compound) must be considered. A field guide, usually mounted on a pantograph on the right side of the animation stand, is often used to help plot motion on the compound from one field size to another. The field guide is calibrated from a 1-field size (which is one inch wide and has a 16 mm or 35 mm aspect ratio, depending on the film shot), to a 12-field size which is 12 inches wide. While cel animation experts say "never go smaller than a 4-field size," photoanimators have successfully gone as small as a 1-field size. And as previously mentioned, innovations such as Comcorps aerial-image device that "widens" the image on 35 mm slides give the photoanimator even greater creative freedom.

But regardless of what field size you use, the field guide plays an important role in helping the animator plot his or her moves with great precision. A good example of how the use of a field guide can help the animator involves the animation of an 8 x 10-inch photograph of a ballet company. In the first scene, the animator wishes to highlight a group of dancers towards the back of the photograph (covered within a 3-field area). He then wants to move from these dancers to the entire ballet company, covered within a 10-field area. If the first scene is in the north (upper middle) part of the field guide, he will have to plot a move that takes the center of the lens (depicted by the stylus on the pantograph) south (toward the center), and up in a slow zoom to reveal the entire 8 x 10 photo, until the stylus is centered in the 10-field area.

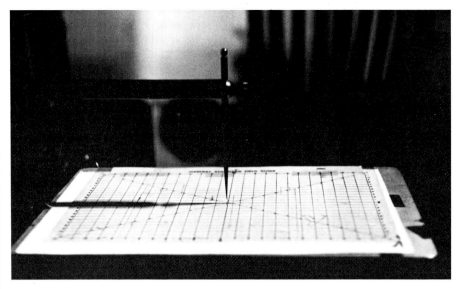

The field guide on the pantograph (side-mounted on the animation stand), aids in plotting all moves on the animation stand. As the field position on the stand changes, the stylus moves to indicate the new position on the field guide.

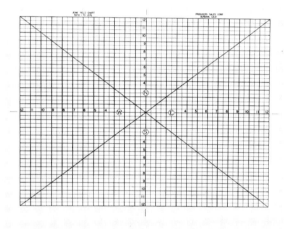

The field guide. (Courtesy of Producers Sales Corporation.)

When you use photo-animation, you can use a picture, such as this ballet company, to show overall and close-up views by changing the field size. In this case, the camera initially covers a small group and then zooms out to reveal the entire company.

When the necessary field sizes are determined and all other decisions on shooting are made, the information is entered on the exposure sheet. This sheet is a frame-by-frame instruction guide for the cameraman, showing all camera and compound moves, including camera exposure control for dissolves, fades, cuts and other scene transitions.

In short, the exposure sheet is a visual representation or blueprint of how the film will look in terms of the camera motion and exposure. Where the **bar sheet** is a visual display of the sound track, the **exposure sheet** is a visual display of the filmed action. The exposure sheet is essential for a

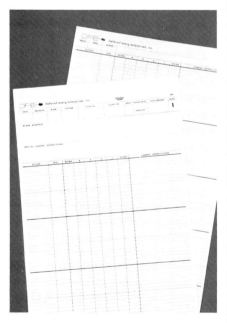

The exposure sheet contains all the information for the animation stand cameraman. It is used as a "blueprint" for the film that will result.
(© Depatie-Freleng Enterprises)

precise filming of the art or photography on the stand and is one of the reasons why most animation can be filmed on a one-to-one shooting ratio. That is, one foot of exposed film to one foot of final, completed film.

When all the art to be used in a photoanimated film is labeled scene-to-scene and plotted on an exposure sheet, it's ready to be filmed. At this point there are a few things you need to know for filming on an animation stand, particularly when filming still photos or art. For example, when you move from one point to another, it's important to understand the "slowing-in" or "slowing-out" process called calculating a fairing. All motion on an animation stand requires a smoothing in and out so that it does not appear to jerk in and out of place. For example, professional cel animators know that when a character pitches a ball, the arm must "slow-in" and "slow-out" of the motion to create the right illusion. And similarly, a pan across a photo or art requires the same care.

Another important point to remember is that zooms cannot be done arbitrarily because there's a difference between the real and apparent speed of a zoom. A 48-frame zoom from a 20 field to a 10 field will appear slower than the same 48-frame zoom from a 20 field to a 5 field. The first zoom (20 to 10) has a 2:1 ratio. The second zoom (20 to 5) has a 4:1 ratio. This indicates a different ratio for the increased image which means that apparent speed is determined not only by frame length but also by the ratio between field sizes.

To plot a move from one point to another, it's necessary to make a line diagram that indicates the spaced increments between the beginning and ending points for a pan or zoom. This is called calibration. Notice that the increments are spaced closer together at the two ends and wider apart in the middle. This "slowing-in" and "slowing-out" process is done so that the viewer's eye can more gradually adjust to the starting and stopping of motion. As you can see in the example, this diagram is often drawn on the peg hole strip that's taped to the top of the artwork to indicate the incremental movements of the animation stand and ending points.

A photoanimator must also be sensitive to scene transitions, particularly when there are in-camera dissolves, fades, out-of-focus transitions, and so forth. All scene transitions, which help to make a smooth and artistic film, must be preselected on the exposure sheet down to each frame number on the frame counter. Cuts that end or begin a scene can be held for a few seconds on the subject to allow some length in case the filmmaker wants to change from the cut to a lab dissolve or some other transition.

With all this motion and camera detail, the animator should remember that proper exposure must be maintained throughout the filming process. Photographic animation is time-consuming, as is cel animation, and frequent meter readings must be taken to check the exposure because the light source may change as the lamps burn for long periods of time. Often, a series of scenes are shot during a session, so if the exposure does not stay constant, the film may have to be "exposure adjusted" or timed scene for scene in a lab. However, when you use tungsten-halogen lamps, the exposure change because of aging is usually inconsequential.

Photographic animation is a very effective technique when done with artistry and finesse. It's also very highly regarded by those who have had a special communication problem to solve on film and have no other answer. Some filmmakers, such as New York's Francis Lee of Film Planning Associates and Al Stahl of Al Stahl Animated, specialize in photoanimation. Francis Lee specializes in large- or standard-format art and black-and-white photography for the production of artistic films for television, educational and business use, and Al Stahl is known for creating motion pictures from slide images, but they both work the spectrum of the photoanimation field with many film festival awards to their credit.

Photoanimation is a technique that has been used, as previously mentioned, for the "breathing of life" into archive photography or great art from centuries past. It has been used extensively in film titles, theatrical trailers, short films, and television spots. An excellent example of its effectiveness is apparent in a scene from the New York trip of Butch Cassidy and the Sundance Kid, in the movie of that name, where a collection of photographs (shot one frame at a time) are used to depict their happy and exciting moments. Photoanimation can be a refreshing break from live action and, in this example, the use of photographic prints rendered in sepia tones created a very special mood.

Three-Dimensional Animation

Three-dimensional animation includes clay figures, puppets, cutouts or any other subject matter that must be moved by hand instead of drawn on a cel or flat surface. An important point to keep in mind prior to working in a three-dimensional mode is that all movement will be recorded by the camera, including camera shake or other vibration, so the beginning animator should be careful to build a rigid set and background. Also make sure that the camera and mount are stable so that no vibrations are recorded during the filming. The lights should remain in place throughout the scene, so the lighting must be planned ahead of time. All action should be preplanned as well, so that scenes can be done in one take. This type of animation is exceedingly time-consuming and takes much patience until the animator gets the knack of it.

The process for three-dimensional animation is exactly the same as for cel work. A script is storyboarded, the dialogue is recorded ahead of time on bar sheets, and all movement is plotted on an exposure sheet. A beginning animator often works with three-dimensional animation because it doesn't require the time-consuming preparation of artwork. It's a good idea to try basic animation in this technique using simple objects such as match sticks, buttons, or clay figures to learn how motion is filmed. After trying these simpler objects, puppets or some other creative forms can be tried. Remember that concept of "slowing in and out" discussed in the photoanimation section? Well, it's used in this mode as well because the same laws of motion apply. If objects, limbs, or other moving things are not eased in and out of motion they appear to jerk in and out of place. Movements should be made using small increments at first, leading to larger moves at the middle point of motion, and smaller moves again as the motion comes to a stop.

Animating Objects

Success with the animation of three-dimensional objects is largely dependent upon the planning of everything in advance down to the last detail, as mentioned previously. Animation of this kind is not particularly difficult and most of the problems encountered will be related to the size, shape, and color of the objects you animate and the types of movements they make. If you want to move an object two inches, for example, make a chart that shows the object's path divided into increments, with appropriate eases at the beginning and at the end of the move. This chart or guide can then be taped down near the object that moves, but out of the camera field. In animating letters which unscramble, for example, each letter's path should be planned in this way. A trick in doing this is shooting the unscramble backwards: Run the film through the camera with the shutter closed for the length of the effect. Align the titles in the desired final order, set the film direction in reverse, and proceed to scramble the letters one increment at a time in the desired pattern. Such reverse shooting of an animation sequence requires a camera with the same registration in reverse and forward, to avoid frame line jumps.

Another creative use of three-dimensional objects is to change the shape or size of the object, instead of moving it from one point to another. This idea was used by a studio in New York City in a television commercial for Widmer Wine. The beginning sequence shows a bottle of wine from which a little red heart pours. Live action footage follows to show couples enjoying the wine—promoting the idea that the wine is associated with happy, romantic moments. The ending repeats the bottle pouring out a heart. This concept was executed by using three-dimensional stop-motion animation. First, the sequence was designed in two dimensions using standard cel animation. Then, a pencil test was made to assure the proper movement, size, and spatial relationships. Next, the cels were given to a model maker who specializes in forms for animation, and each cel became a three-dimensional form. Using lucite, eighteen hearts were made, each one a little larger than the other. By filming each heart separately and substituting another heart that was a little bigger in the same position, the heart on film appears to be expanding or filling out as the wine bottle is tipped. This is just one example of how three-dimensional animation can be used to meet your communications needs—only your imagination limits the creative possibilities.

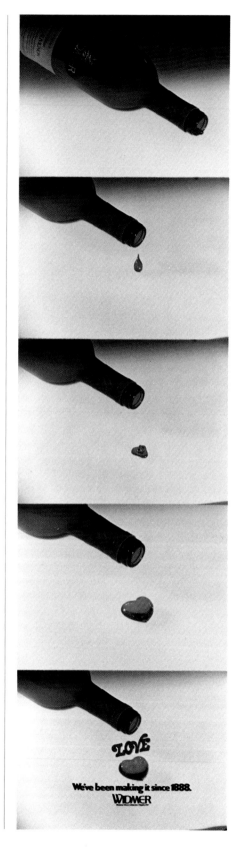

These frames, from a Widmer Wine spot, show the use of a stop-motion special effects technique with three-dimensional objects.
Agency: Hutchins/Y&R.
Production House: Mike Nebbia Productions.
Animation Director: John Gati.

Puppet Animation

After enough experience in animating objects is obtained, or at least to the point where the animator feels comfortable enough to try puppets, there are a few basics to remember about puppets. Remember that each second of elapsed time is 24 frames. Much can be done in one second if the motion increments are large, but very little motion needs to be recorded if none is needed. The eye can pick up motion in one twenty-fourth of a second, but will accept fairly fluid motion in one-twelfth of a second increments, or two-frame increments per motion, as in most cel animation.

Much of professional puppet animation is done with wooden puppets because the wood is rigid and wooden puppets can take much handling with minor paint retouching. The beginning puppet animator might want to try some toy plastic puppets with movable joints that take much wear and tear. If you want to try to make puppets from scratch, keep them simple and stylized instead of lifelike. Lifelike puppets, unless they're made extremely well, like the examples from professional clay animator Bob Gardiner's studio, can have a rather ghoulish appearance that diminishes the intended effect. If puppets are designed to look and act like the little jointed characters they are, the animated film will have a more refreshing charm.

Although puppets can also be made of wax, wax will soften under hot lights. Clay is also difficult to work with because it usually crumbles and does not retain its shape well. One technique that works well in clay, however, is a metamorphosis, or the changing of one shape into another. For example, a giant clay box can change into many monkeys, slowly at first and then with rapidity.

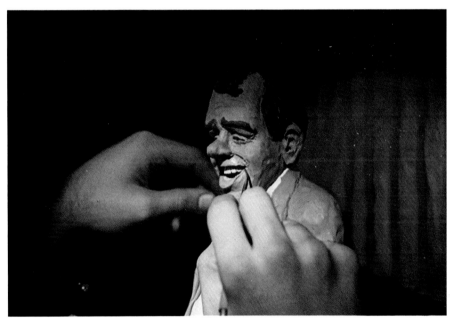

Here are two fine examples of clay animation, created for two films by professional clay animator Bob Gardiner, the Ted Hallock Advertising Agency, and the Film Loft. The soccer players (top) were featured in a film created for the Portland Parks Department. The stand-up clay comic (bottom) was done for a film called "Keep Oregon Livable." (Courtesy of Bob Gardiner)

Modeling clay or Plasticine clay is excellent to use because it's very pliable and comes in many colors that add to the attractiveness of the clay figure changing shape. The figure must be well balanced so it won't fall over during filming. To prevent this, the bottom portion should be made heavy enough to support the whole figure. If a lot of motion is planned for a clay figure, make sure the pieces that move are thick enough to hold their position between exposures. If the figure changes expression, it's a good idea to mold these pieces separately and stick them on at the appropriate time so that the main body won't be changed.

Regardless of what type of puppet you choose, always consider the amount of space available. If you make the puppets too large, the accompanying background and props will have to be just as large to accommodate them. An appropriate scale is one that is small enough to fit into the allotted space, but large enough to show facial expression on the puppet, which should change, particularly if there is dialogue. An excellent example of the enchanting quality that puppets can create is the film HANSEL AND GRETEL, produced by Michael Myerberg Productions. The beauty of this film lies in the very smooth, flowing action of the sensitively designed puppets.

From HANSEL AND GRETEL. Gretel's plastic face has expression and character with human qualities, while still retaining a "doll-like" appearance. Note the detail in hair and clothing which helps to create the feeling of life. (Courtesy of Michael Meyerberg. © New Trends Association, Inc.)

Paper Cutouts

Paper cutout animation is one of the most elementary and economical types of animation, and is also the type that most young students begin with. The young children pictured in this section are from an elementary school class that experimented with basic animation techniques. This is an excellent example of how valuable animation can be as a teaching tool. Their teacher, Mrs. Susan Lerner, who is now principal at the Lake Stickney Elementary School in Alderwood Manor, Washington, has found that children experimenting with animation experience more than ordinary growth in reading and writing skills, oral expression, appreciation of literature and music, as well as social studies and science. They also develop

additional planning and organization skills, self-confidence, and the ability to get along with other children. Mrs. Lerner's students went through the complete planning process, including writing stories and scripts, drawing cutouts and backgrounds, recording narration and sound, and the actual filming with a super 8 movie camera.

In addition to teaching children important skills, paper cutout animation is also effective for training purposes. Imagine a lesson in chess using paper cutout chessmen. The cutouts can be moved about the chessboard to show possibilities for each turn. Paper cutouts can also be used to indicate weather conditions, showing storm fronts and various meteorological data. The possibilities are virtually limitless.

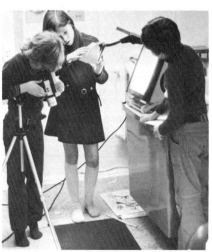

(top left) Washington students write stories and scripts for their animated films. (bottom left) Students set up for an animation session using overhead projectors as a light source. (top right) Cutting out drawings for the sequence. (bottom right) The director reads from a film plan and the photographer shoots as the animator moves the drawing. (Courtesy of Susan Lerner)

Slide Animation

Slide animation in multi-image presentations is yet another technique that offers numerous communications advantages. Although some think the rapid cycling of slide projectors produces the same effect as a movie, slide animation actually offers some distinct advantages that make it dramatically different from a movie. You just can't duplicate the smoothness of a motion picture. Instead, the creator must do careful planning because he relies on "after images" in the viewer's mind that subconsciously connect the motion between the images on a slide. This offers an advantage because a producer has the freedom to alter the time intervals between images depending on what effect he wants to achieve.

Richard Shipps, president of DD&B Studios in Detroit, who produces multi-image programs daily, confirms the advantages that slide animation offers. Shipps says, "As a producer, your options are almost limitless . . ." He continues, "if something doesn't work, we pull it out and insert something else. This ability to be creative spontaneously, of course, is an advantage the motion picture animator doesn't have." And with slides, you have the additional advantage of using any format you desire, instead of the standard three-to-four format of 16 mm movie film.

Producers Alan Koslowski and Jim Bunkleman echo these sentiments. At Synergetic Media Inc. in Hollywood, they produced a 30-projector multi-image demonstration program for Audio Visual Laboratories to promote the capabilities of their new Eagle multi-image programming computer. This masterpiece of imagery, REFLECTIONS IN A CRYSTAL WIND, was significant not only because of the quality of the images (see samples on right), but because of the animation rate—up to 20 slides per second, a feat made possible by the Eagle unit.

Some of the sample slides shown here are offset ¼ frame because they were projected from different banks and had to register perfectly in the center of the screen.

The dancer was shot on a black stage on 35 mm motion picture film and transferred to slides on a compound animation stand. This transfer was calculated to an accuracy of 1/2000th of an inch in order to keep her aligned as the image moved back and forth between different slide banks.

These five slides are taken from a sequence which used every other frame of the original motion picture footage. We selected every other slide to show the range of her movement; therefore, you're seeing every fourth frame of the original film. The end result is exciting and dramatic animation that has numerous applications.

For more information on slide animation, refer to Kodak's publication, **IMAGES, IMAGES, IMAGES—The Book of Programmed Multi-Image Production (S-12).**

Some animation "magic" from REFLECTIONS IN A CRYSTAL WIND where animation rates of up to 20 slides per second produce very dramatic results.

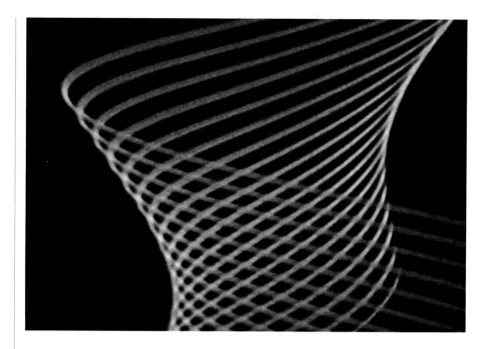

Here's an example of an abstract raster pattern generated on Computer Image's "Scanimate" video animation equipment. (Courtesy of Computer Image)

Computer Animation

Many of the animated special effects you see in television commercials and logo identifications are created by a computer system that can produce an unending variety of effective and exciting visual effects. Although this type of animation is fairly new, interest has grown tremendously since Computer Image Corporation, originally created by artist/engineer Lee Harrison, developed an electronic animation system in 1968 called Scanimate.

The Scanimate animation system involves the use of a computer and electronic equipment that create original shapes and designs by manipulating input images. The input images can be rolled, twisted, undulated, etc, and then colored by means of an electronic system that identifies variable densities of the gray scale and codes each level with a different color. Thus, any level of gray can be coded or recoded for a specific color or combination of colors.

The input image is usually black-and-white flat line art on transparent sheets such as KODALITH Film sheets. "These sheets are the counterpart of cels used in conventional animation," say the Computer Image people. But, there is one very important difference that this company emphasizes: A single sheet is equivalent to dozens, or even hundreds, of conventional cels. What this means to the client is that production schedules and costs are greatly reduced because the computer's animation is much less time-consuming than the animation created through numerous hand-drawn cels. The result is a form of animation that somewhat resembles cel animation, although it does not have the careful, intricate line movement of the hand-drawn cels.

The actual procedure for making a computer animation sequence is not very complicated; in fact, no knowledge of computers is required for a client to understand how the Scanimate system works, according to a Computer Image spokesman. After the black-and-white artwork is transferred to a KODALITH Film sheet, the sheet is placed in front of a television camera to allow the operator to watch the image of the artwork as he moves the appropriate knobs and dials for the desired effect. Each knob or dial affects a specific change in the image, such as position, size, intensity, duration of the sequence, and the animation itself. It is also possible to divide a whole image into component parts, with each part independently animated. When the operator decides how the image will move, he adjusts the controls to establish the length of the sequence and the position on the screen where he wants the image to begin and end.

After these steps are done, the operator is ready to animate the image with a limitless variety of effects and movements. As the image moves from the beginning to ending position, the computer executes whatever animation techniques have been programmed. The sequence can be repeated and changed as many times as necessary until the operator is satisfied with the results.

As briefly mentioned earlier, the transparent areas of the sheet are masked with variable densities of gray scale so that each area transmits a different amount of light.

A commercial spot created by Dolphin Productions for Pepto-Bismol. Agency: Benton & Bowles. Producers/Directors: Dolphin Productions.

When the animation is complete, the colorizer portion of the computer "reads" the light levels, then assigns a different color to each area.

There are five red-blue-green mixing controls that the operator can use to paint each area of the image any color desired. After the animation is colored, the final completed image is shown on a second viewing screen in full color. The abstract raster pattern generated on Computer Image's Scanimate suggests the versatility of movement, shapes, and color.

Dolphin Productions. a company that also utilizes Computer Image's system, produces computerized graphics and custom visuals for clients such as Freshen-Up Gum, Singer, United Way of America, and Pepto-Bismol. The Pepto-Bismol example shows the capabilities of the computerized system; the body of the main character is distorted by the computer to visually emphasize the way his stomach feels. Dolphin Productions has also found computer animation to be effective for educational purposes, as well. Certain segments of CBS's **The Red River,** a documentary about heart functions, were created by this company with highly effective results.

The future for computer animation appears to be unlimited. Currently, a newer animation system called Caesar (Computer Animated Episodes Using Single Axis Rotation), also developed by

An operator at the console of the CAESAR system. (Courtesy of Computer Image)

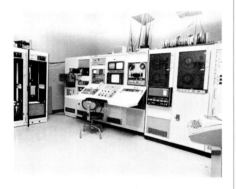

An overall view of CAESAR; two art input camera boxes are on the left, the operator's console is in the center, and the computer bank is on the right.

the Computer Image Corporation, is capable of producing character animation. This system is more complex than the Scanimate system and allows for a more detailed manipulation of parts. In fact, it even has the ability to produce lip-sync with up to seven different mouth shapes to choose from. The Caesar system follows some of the same steps used in conventional cel animation. The production begins with a storyboard that resembles a comic strip. Then a script is written and a sound track is recorded before the animating begins. Similar to a key animator for cel animation, the operator animates key motion points, encoding the information into the computer. Then the computer, like the in-betweener in cel animation, fills in all the remaining motion, frame by frame. The television screen that the image is viewed on is divided into seven different sections that

can be controlled independently. This means that a cartoon character's head, arms, legs, tail, etc, can all be manipulated separately and then combined to create a fully animated character. Also, if more than one character is desired, additional characters can be keyed over the scene in successive passes of ten or more. When the scene is completed, it can be played back and reviewed before final taping. The entire production time for a 30-second spot, using the Caesar system, is approximately one week.

Computer animation offers yet another animation alternative. Its popularity is based on the fact that it takes less time to create than other types of animation, produces dramatic special effects, and offers an effective communications tool for numerous commercial and educational purposes.

This animated character was created by Computer Image's CAESAR system for a public service spot for the Department of Agriculture.

Cel Animation

If you can envision an actor's studio sometime prior to the coming of motion pictures, you might see the teacher or coach shouting "project, project" to the student. The student would then breathe in a lot of air, and go deep inside the chest to deliver a line with exaggerated force and vitality, and at the same time, effect mannerisms and gestures that were bigger than life.

Imagine now, that same young actor in the silent era of film. The voice would not be heard, but the audience, just like the back row of the theatre audience, had to read the message and feel the waves of power and force.

Now, visualize Chaplin's movements as the little tramp. Every move, manner, gesture is crystal clear. There is no mistaking what he is doing from scene to scene. If you can imagine all this, you have learned the first lesson in cel animation. Former Disney animator Art Babbitt, who is now working and teaching at the Richard Williams studio, expresses the idea this way: "Exaggerate until you think you've reached the limit," he says, "then exaggerate some more."

Art Babbitt and most other professionals who are highly skilled in the technique of animation claim that you cannot put

An early and superb example of character development is Walt Disney's THE THREE LITTLE PIGS, 1933, a film which also exemplified the early use of color in animated cartoons.
(© Walt Disney Productions)

enough exaggerated, detailed motion into a character: "No matter how much you've put in, there's still more to do," says Babbitt. An excellent example of detailed character motion is Disney's THE THREE LITTLE PIGS, which Babbitt worked on. All three pigs look the same, but their individual, exaggerated body movements give them separate, unique personalities that enable the audience to tell one pig from the other. Another more recent example is Richard Williams' film, RAGGEDY ANN AND ANDY, released in 1977. Babbitt also worked on this film in addition to teaching many of the young animators who worked on it, too. The character movement is superbly detailed, as the drawing of the camel and the cel of Raggedy Ann suggest.

Richard Williams adds a few details to the animated camel drawn by Art Babbit for Williams' 1977 film, RAGGEDY ANN AND ANDY.

Raggedy Ann, from the beautifully animated RAGGEDY ANN AND ANDY, 1977, directed by Richard Williams.
(© 1977 The Bobbs-Merrill Company, Inc.)

To illustrate how much work goes into a single sequence that has been done well, the same artists who did the cover of this book were asked to take us from storyboard to camera ready cels in the following pages. But the first step before you even think about storyboarding is to ask yourself: Why animation? One reason is because animation offers a very human element that appeals to the emotions of the audience. It can, therefore, be more persuasive for some purposes than live action is. A good example of this is a Chevron commercial created by Kurtz and Friends in Los Angeles. The company is transformed into a friendly dinosaur that eats slices of "bread" representing the company's expenditures, as a voice-over explains where each fraction of money goes.

Another reason to use animation is because it can show and do things that other media cannot. Animation takes over where live action leaves off. Remember, cel animation isn't just cartoons. It's elaborate technical motion . . . the insides of an operating jet turbine showing fuel flow and exhaust in fine detail . . . the human circulatory system showing the intricacies of heart-valve action . . . a rocket launch that exists only theoretically. Now that we've established that an animated film can be an effective communications tool, let's go through the steps involved in creating such a film.

One of Kurtz & Friends Clio award winners, this commercial spot for Chevron is an effective, creative example of how dynamic animation can be.

The Storyboard

Once you have a script, the next step is to storyboard it. A storyboard is simply the visualization of every key scene or sequence in the production so that a viewer can see the central action in the story. Most big-budget, live-action feature films are storyboarded prior to production, as are virtually all television commercials. And the storyboard stage is even more important for animated films because of the additional need to visualize in advance. Therefore, all animated films should be storyboarded prior to production.

In our first example we see the sequence of motion for an animated segment. It can be described as follows: There are two elves. Elf A is shown in frame one, screen right. In frame two, we see Elf A motioning for Elf B to play leapfrog (at this point we just see the arm wave and do not know why Elf A is beckoning). In frame three, Elf B leapfrogs over Elf A, and in the fourth and final frame, we see Elf B gleefully standing at screen left after his leap.

The storyboard tells the animated story in a series of key scenes, much the same as a comic strip does.

Do not confuse these four "sequence of motion" frames with "animation extremes," because they are too coarse and much too general to be extremes. A good example of an extreme would be a pendulum bob that swings from left to right. When the pendulum

has reached as far left as possible we have one extreme and another when it has reached as far right as possible. This is not the case here. The storyboard begins with Elf A who appears first. The most extreme character pose is for Elf B, who comes on the screen farther to the left than Elf A. What we see in a storyboard, and specifically in an animation storyboard, is a "visual highlight" of the script. The storyboard will show enough information for the viewer to follow the entire course of action.

The Path of Action

Creating the path of action is the next step. Compare the path of action with the storyboard. Immediately, you can see that the path of action gives you different information. It does not tell as much as the storyboard tells about the story, but it gives you

an idea of the action required in the sequence of motion and shows the most extreme character poses in the sequence. The elves are already labeled A and B in the description for the storyboard, so you know that Elf A is first on screen, motions to B, bends over and allows B to jump over. The path of action tells you that in order to properly simulate life motion, you need to give Elf B a lot of space for a running start

to "ease him in" and additional room to "ease him out" at the end of the sequence, instead of plopping him down and stopping the action abruptly. You shouldn't just divide the motion into 12 equal parts and draw equally divided segments. It's important to "ease" or "slow" a moving object or character in and out of its extreme. This is similar to the pan fairings discussed in the photoanimation section.

The path of action gives you an idea of the action in the sequence and shows the most extreme character poses.

After you complete the path of action, it's a good time to think about the field size you're going to cover (laying out the background, etc). Most animation is shot within a 4 to 12-field range. As mentioned in the previous section on photographic animation, the field size and motion of the sequence is planned with the field guide on the animation stand, such as the 12-field guide shown.

As the scene begins, Elf A starts the action with his motion, per the storyboard, and once stooping, stops his own action. But Elf B continues to move across the screen, making it necessary to pan or follow him with the camera, to be sure he's on screen all the time that he's in motion. To make it more interesting, you might also consider zooming back a little to reveal more of the background and prevent the illusion that the elf is lost in the bottom of some far-off giant forest. So, using the field guide you can create a field guide overlay similar to the one shown, that shows what field sizes and effects you've chosen. The choice of field size and any camera moves is made according to how large or small you want the image on the screen. It's an arbitrary decision that depends on your own sense of proportion and taste. This field guide overlay shows that the animator plans to start framing in a 9½ field.

As the overlay indicates, the field stays the same as the east pan begins at point A. The pan continues in a 9½ field to point B. At B the up-zoom begins and the field size gradually moves from a 9½- to a 12-field size which is 19-field steps away from the center on the field guide (each rectangular division is called a field step). The maximum field size in this sequence is 12, a size often

used by most animators. The visual result is as follows: The camera picks up on Elf A in a 9½ field. Elf B appears, leaps over Elf A and the animator pans east to follow him until Elf A is out of the frame. As Elf B continues to move the animator begins to zoom out and the sequence ends with Elf B. The path of action shows all the key drawings in the sequence series. The field guide overlay tells how much of the information will be covered and how. This information will later be transferred to an exposure sheet for shooting when the number of character movements is established.

The field guide overlay indicates the field size information decided on for the film.

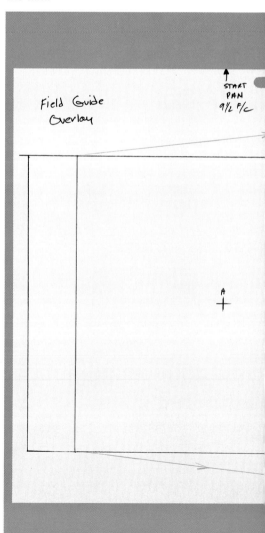

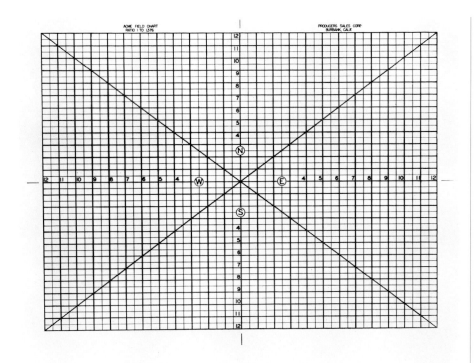

The field guide is exactly what the name implies. It is a guide used to determine the field position for the film. The guide is placed on the animation stand compound, under the platen, so that the cameraman can look through the lens and determine what field size is appropriate for the artwork used. A duplicate of the guide is usually placed on the pantograph to further assist the cameraman; the stylus on the pantograph, which moves above the field guide, represents the center of the camera lens and provides a visual record of field position movements on the stand.

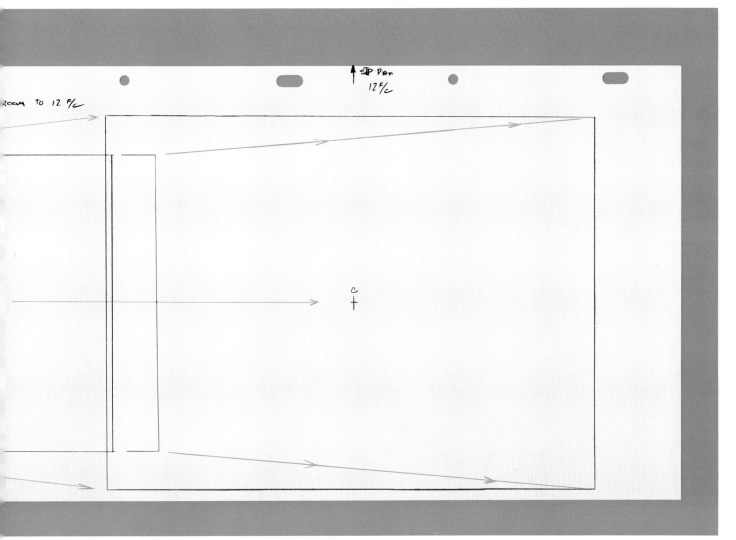

Laying Out the Background

Laying out the background is an important stage in an animation production because it's at this point that the overall look and mood of the film is determined. The versatility of most animation stands should be considered when an artist lays out the background. Imagine a three-dimensional mode of motion as you plan the artwork. The compound on an animation stand has the ability, in most cases, to move in all east-west-north-south directions and in between, and can actually spin and tilt on more complex setups. The registration pegs on the compound can travel in east-west directions, sometimes in motions opposing each other as in a multi-plane scene where a train and an automobile might be in the foreground and a plane in the background, all moving at different speeds. In this case, the artist's background rough layout reflects the decision to zoom out— notice that the artwork widens on the right.

In the first background rough for the elf sequence, the artist created an elaborate but subdued background. In this case, a relatively decorative background helps create atmosphere, but does not overwhelm the characters. In the case of limited-motion animation where only parts of the body move, a highly decorative background is more important because it has to do more than simply complement the animation. In an animation studio, a cleaned-up version, a one-color composite, and then a full-color composite are made for approval by the film's director.

A background, as shown in this rough, should support the animated images on the cel, not overwhelm them. In full-motion animation, the background plays a subdued role, complementing the cel art. In limited motion, the background is more pronounced and is sometimes as important an emphasis as the cel art.

Once the background is designed, a cleaned up version is used for approval by the film's director and/or producer.

This full-color composite showing the background and overlay gives the film's director and staff a clearer idea of what the finished watercolor will look like.

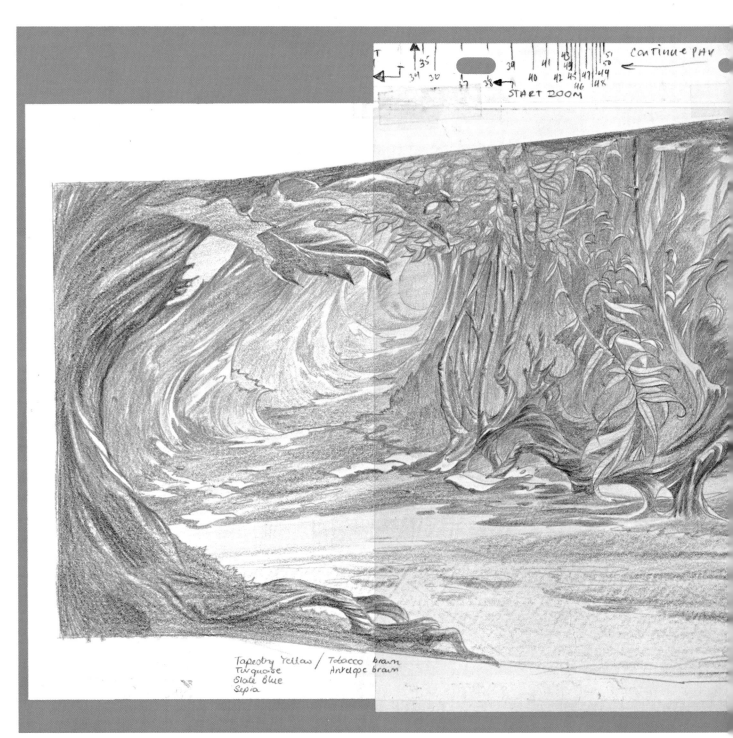

Usually, a comprehensive is used for color matching. The cel used here is a nonproduction cel for color matching purposes only.

44

Examine the comprehensive of the background with a nonproduction cel of one of the elves placed on top of it for color matching. Notice that the background colors are listed at the bottom of the artwork for future reference. This type of color comprehensive is not usually done by most studios and independent animators because it's expensive and time-consuming. The Disney studio is an exception; color comprehensive backgrounds are often used on a Disney innovation known as the Leica reel (named after the camera of that name), a reel of film composed of pencil tests, completed segments, sketches and roughs at various stages of production so that the director can see how the film is shaping up.

The finished background with the foreground overlay shown here is now camera-ready for the animation stand.

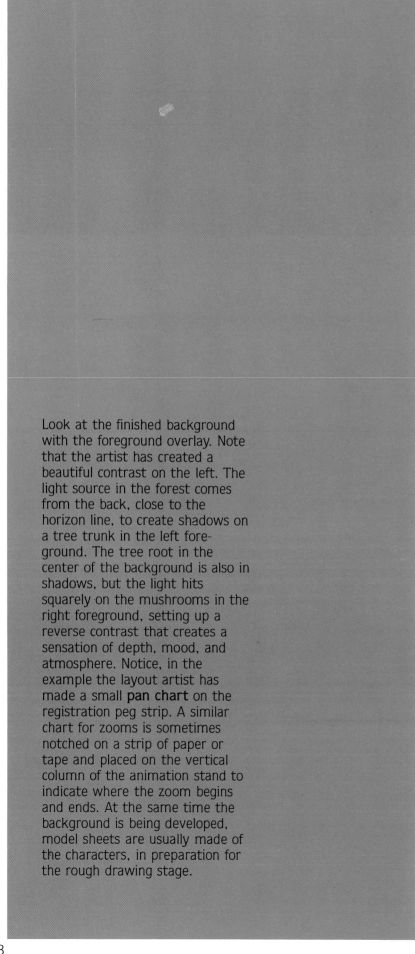

Look at the finished background with the foreground overlay. Note that the artist has created a beautiful contrast on the left. The light source in the forest comes from the back, close to the horizon line, to create shadows on a tree trunk in the left foreground. The tree root in the center of the background is also in shadows, but the light hits squarely on the mushrooms in the right foreground, setting up a reverse contrast that creates a sensation of depth, mood, and atmosphere. Notice, in the example the layout artist has made a small **pan chart** on the registration peg strip. A similar chart for zooms is sometimes notched on a strip of paper or tape and placed on the vertical column of the animation stand to indicate where the zoom begins and ends. At the same time the background is being developed, model sheets are usually made of the characters, in preparation for the rough drawing stage.

Rough Drawings

After a character is designed and approved, the designer makes up a **model sheet** of the newly born character, such as the model sheets shown on this page from Fleischer's GULLIVER'S TRAVELS, 1939, and the one on the opposite page from Richard William's forthcoming animated feature film, THE THIEF AND THE COBBLER. Sometimes a model sheet will show the size of all the characters in relation to each other. Other model sheets show a single character at various angles.

These two Gabby model sheets, from Fleischer's GULLIVER'S TRAVELS, show the shape, expression, and movement in the character. The pencil notes describe further details for the animation staff by the character designer.

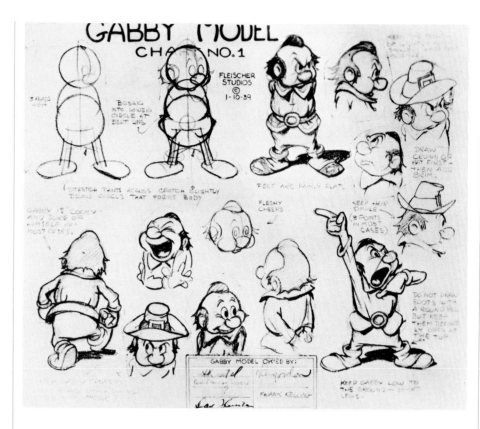

The first model sheet for The Mad
Holy Old Witch Of The Desert
Mountain, a character in Richard
Williams' forthcoming animated
feature film THE THIEF AND THE COBBLER.

When the animator has a model sheet, background layout, script, and path of action, the next step is to make rough drawings of the complete action. In a studio where there is a clear division of responsibilities, a key animator makes a spacing guide that indicates the action and the in-betweener draws the movements in between indicated by the guide. The end result of this stage should reflect continuity of form and smoothness of motion.

The first step in the rough drawing stage is to draw the beginning extreme of motion on paper with punched holes to fit on the peg bars of the drawing board. (These punched holes should also fit on the peg bars of the animation stand.) When the first drawing is done on the board, the next piece of paper is placed over the pegs. The first drawing can be seen through the top sheet of paper, and the second drawing can be drawn with the motion progression a little more advanced than in the original drawing. In animation, a two frames-per-drawing standard is usually followed, so each drawing represents two frames of film. These rough drawings are

The key animator's spacing guide (to the right of elf pose 10 and 12) gives the in-betweener a fairly accurate idea of how many character movements need to be drawn between the extremes shown.

The same progression, cleaned up to show finer detail and expression, is now ready for the inker or electrostatic copier to transfer the art onto a cel.

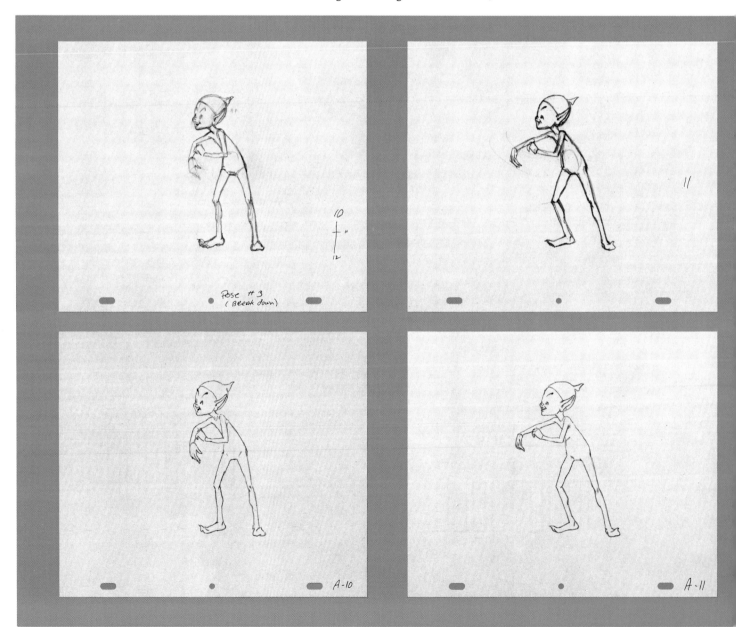

really the blueprints for what will be transferred to the actual cels, via the electrostatic copier or manual inking process. When this sequence is filmed, the drawings on the cels will line up on the animation stand the same way the roughs do on the drawing board. Now the chosen field sizes, pans, and zooms, can be plotted on the exposure sheet (discussed in the photoanimation section from the field overlay), along with the determined number of character movements. This sheet will give the cameraman a frame-by-frame guide for putting the sequence on film.

Cleaning Up

To see the importance of this next stage, compare the rough drawings of Elf A with the cleanups for the same sequence. If you observe closely, you can see the fine detail such as the facial expression and the clean quality of the lines. A tracing process is also used to draw the cleanups. Each drawing in the rough stage is placed on the drawing board with a clean piece of punched paper over it. The animator then "traces" the rough drawing, refining the lines and adding more detail. Even the thickness of a pencil line is critical at this stage. For example, if you trace a line on the left side of the original pencil line in the rough, you should not trace on the right for the next drawing because it will look like a "jiggle" to the viewer of the completed film. The flow of motion can be checked by using a method called "flipping." This method gives a very rough idea of how the action will look on film.

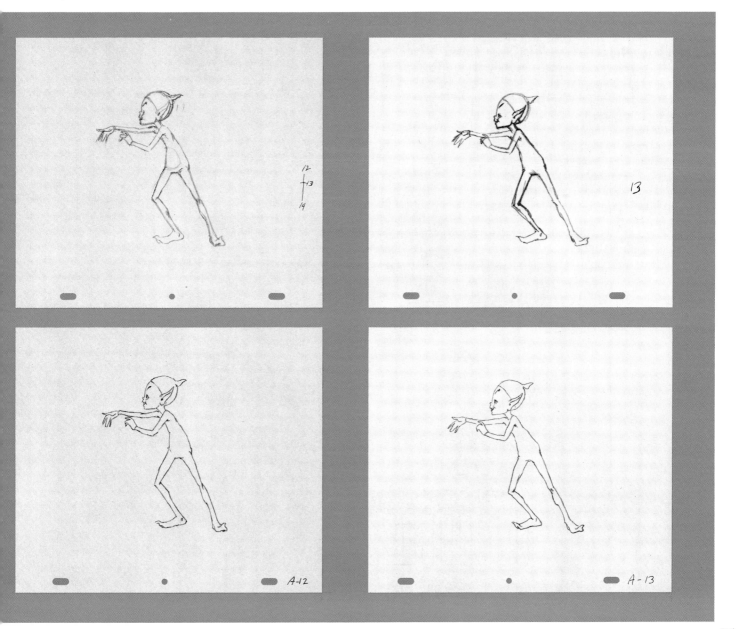

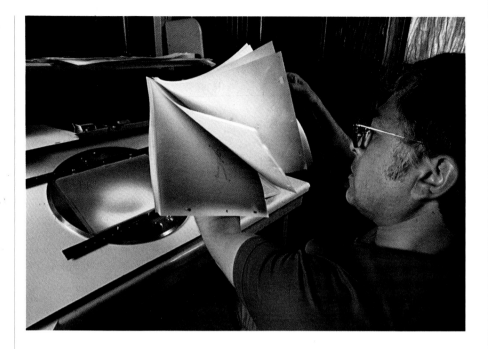

Inking and Opaquing

The tracing process continues
through the inking stage. The
cleanup is placed on the drawing
board and a piece of acetate, with
punched holes, is placed on top of
it. Now, the inker uses any one or
a combination of pens, crayons,
and pencils to trace the cleanup.

The electrostatic copying process
provides an alternative to this
time-consuming inking process.
The copier process used for cels is
basically the same process in an
office copier, but a slight modifica-
tion has been made to accommodate cels instead of paper—the
heating elements have been
cooled down to protect the
acetate cels. The cels are fed
through the machine with the
cleanup paper on the bottom

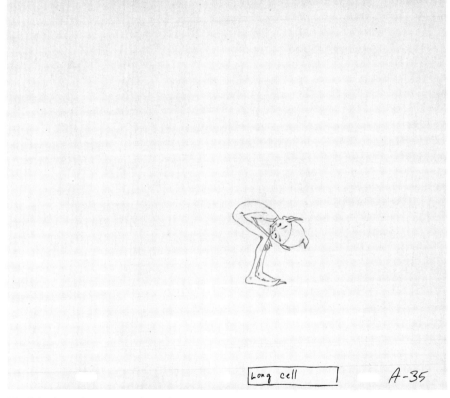

Long cell   A-35

without registration holes punched (the peg holes are punched after the copying has been done and each cel must be registered or "pegged" after punching). Since the copier does not pick up lines that are not firm and black and cannot reproduce large solid black areas, it cannot be used in all situations.

When the inking or electrostating of the cels is done, the next step is to opaque or paint color on the cels in between the lines. This is done on the reverse side of the cel to keep the ink line intact. Cel vinyl paint is most often used and there is a broad range of colors available, including gray tints useful for night scenes, foggy atmosphere, and so forth. The colors you choose should be matched only after they dry; a wet color always appears lighter because it reflects more light. When your colors are chosen and you're ready to opaque the cels, the basic rule to remember is as elementary as a child's lesson for using a coloring book: Stay within the lines! When the painting is done and the cels are dry, they are cleaned, checked, and then moved to the animation stand for filming.

The coloring or opaquing is done on the bottom or underneath side of the cel. The inked lines on the opposite side provide an outline for the painter to use.

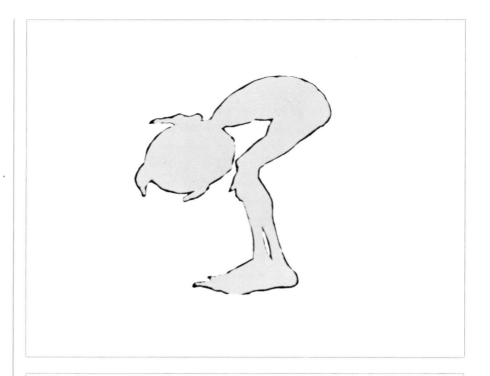

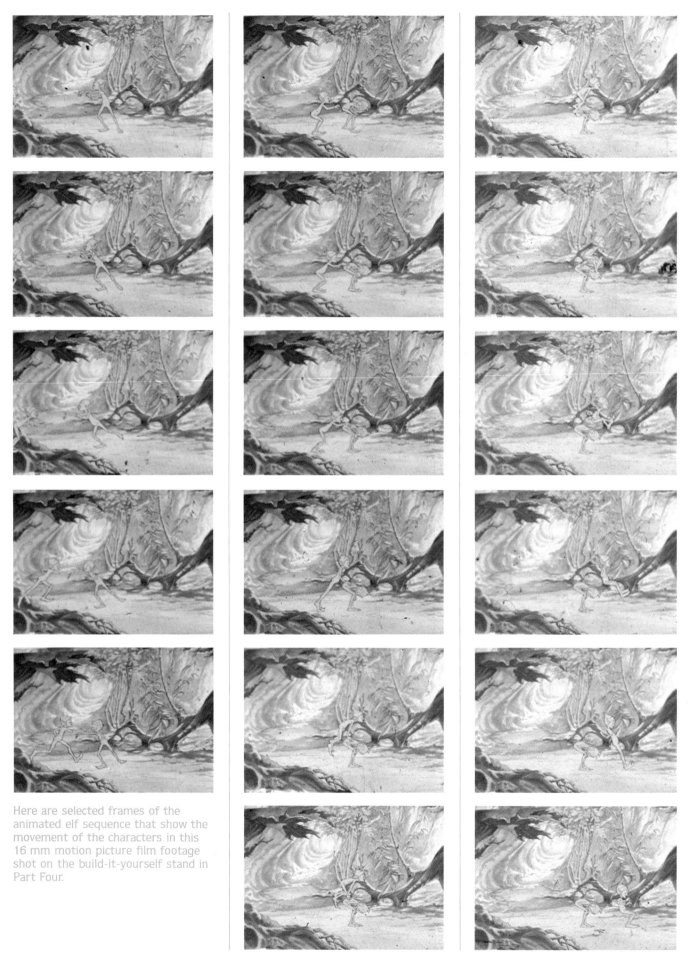

Here are selected frames of the animated elf sequence that show the movement of the characters in this 16 mm motion picture film footage shot on the build-it-yourself stand in Part Four.

PART THREE

The Animation Stand: The Basic Parts and How They Function

The successful production of an animated film requires accurate control of the movements of the camera and artwork, since the slightest inaccuracy will be greatly magnified when the film is projected. Consequently, the animation stand you choose is of prime importance. Historically, there have been two types of animation stands: horizontal and vertical. The horizontal stand is used for large art, three-dimensional objects, and in special cases, such as the system set up by the Comcorps Company in Washington, D.C. (mentioned in the previous section), for aerial image filming of transparencies. But the horizontal stand is limited because of its lack of efficiency and versatility, so the vertical stand has become the accepted standard by most manufacturers.

Most vertical stands are made of high quality steel and aluminum with a square base that supports a vertical track on one or two columns. The camera is mounted on the track, pointing down, and can move up or down to any desired height over the copy area. Although it is possible to accomplish certain types of animation through the use of a tripod, an animation stand helps to ensure professional quality in all phases of the work and effects important economies in production time because it's more stable and doesn't move accidentally. The advantage of camera-in-motion techniques, such as zooms, pans, or tilts, can easily be achieved with most animation stands and you can get the effects without the need for a large number of additional drawings.

Stands range from highly precise and often elaborate pieces of equipment from manufacturers such as Oxberry and Acme to custom-built units constructed for a specific type of animation work. Most professional animation stands will accommodate either a 35 mm or a 16 mm camera, or a combination camera with interchangeable magazines. There are also commercially available stands designed for super 8 movie cameras only. For student or semiprofessional applications, several very light stands have been developed by the Oxberry Company and Ox Products, Inc. For the more serious beginning animator, we suggest that you take a look at the build-it-yourself wooden stand discussed in the next section. This stand has all the basic features that a professional stand has, at a fraction of the cost. It is designed to be built for approximately $400, or about $200 if you don't need the suggested animation disc. If you decide to just build the basic stand for $200 without the disc, consider a tapedown peg bar for about $24 to replace the mounted peg bars on the disc. This will save you about $150 but will also limit your shooting to the north-south or east-west movement of the compound because the peg bars will be taped down. What it all comes down to is choosing the stand with the specific features you need at a cost that's within your budget. Although there are some very inexpensive stands on the market (for several hundred dollars), the simplest, sufficiently professional animation stand available from manufacturers at this time costs about $1,000, with other professional models going up to $100,000 and beyond, depending on how much automation is required. The trade-off on automation in this case involves volume and speed versus cost. The higher cost can be justified if your volume is high enough and your deadlines are consistently tight.

But regardless of what animation stand you may choose to use, there are basic parts on most stands that function the same way. One such part is the compound. The **compound** or artwork table on which you place the art to be photographed can be as simple as a flat, level table. If a flat table is used, you can register pieces of art that follow each other by placing tape at the corners of the first piece so you can line up the ones that follow. Then, you can use more tape to hold down the artwork during the shooting. But even the most elementary compound on an animation stand usually offers a few more features that make registration easier than this. The usual compound or table has **registration peg bars** to keep the cel levels in registration with each other and with the background art, which is also punched for peg registration. The Acme peg system is a West Coast standard, and the Oxberry system is now an East Coast standard. The Disney Studio is the only one that does not use either one of these systems. This studio has its own stands, field sizes, and registration peg system (which is somewhat larger than the Acme or Oxberry systems).

Traveling peg bars are another feature of some compounds that allow for the simulation of movement from one cel to another or from the cel levels to the background. For example, a cel of a boy on a bicycle appears to be static until we shoot the cel cycle over a slow-moving background. The background can move from east to west, or the reverse, by means of traveling peg bars.

In addition to the movement offered by the traveling peg bars, all professional compounds provide for movement in a north-south and east-west direction by the turning of **cranks** that move the compound horizontally. And all complete stands also have vertical columns that allow the camera to move up and down for vertical zooming.

Some compounds also have a **disc** that allows a 360-degree-rotation capability enabling spinning and tilting shots to be executed easily. This disc feature usually includes a glass plate in the center that functions like a light box. If you use transparencies, they can be lighted from underneath this plate for filming.

On all professional and most amateur stand compounds, there is a **platen** over the artwork to hold it down and keep it from curling under the hot lights. The build-it-yourself stand discussed in the next section has a platen that is very much like those found on large stands. The platen must be large enough to accommodate the largest field size to be used. When a platen is not used, or an inadequate one is used during filming, the animator will very often notice cel shadows on the background. This is not only distracting, but ruins the effect of the film. Much care must be taken to keep the artwork flat, clean, and free of fingerprints (which show up glaringly on a finished film). The platen should rest securely on the artwork, but not too tightly; a very heavy platen often produces "Newton's rings" on the cels. If the platen is too loose and shadows form on the background artwork, you can use a thin foam pad as a mat behind the background.

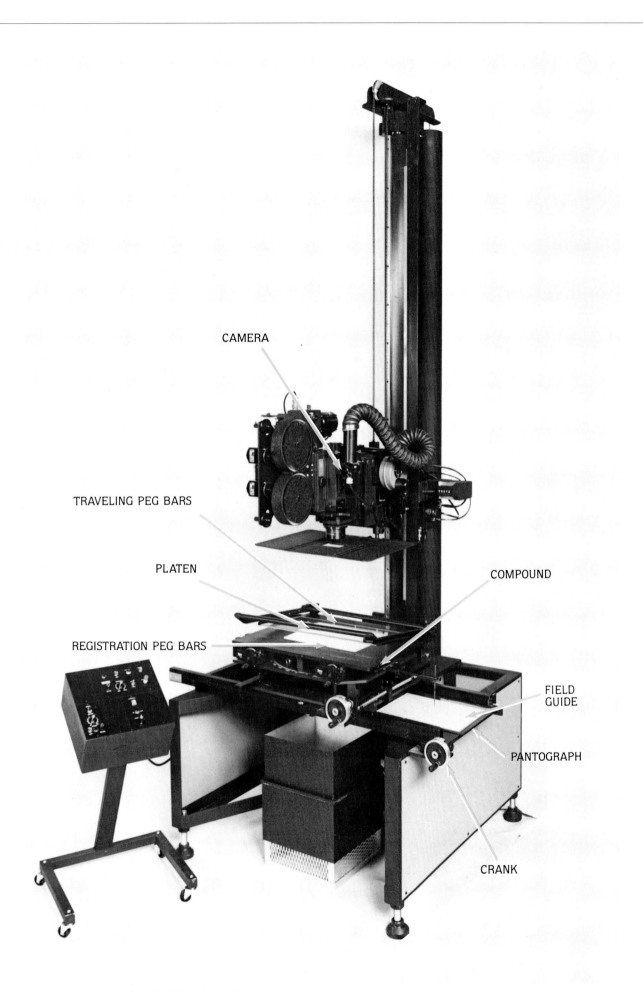

CAMERA

TRAVELING PEG BARS

PLATEN

COMPOUND

REGISTRATION PEG BARS

FIELD GUIDE

PANTOGRAPH

CRANK

OXBERRY FILMMAKER 16 mm Animation Stand and Camera

(Courtesy of Oxberry Co.)

The **pantograph**, mounted on the right side of the compound, usually consists of a stylus mounted over the center of a flat table with a field guide on it that refers to the field of shooting for the artwork. The **field guide**, already discussed in Part Two, is used as a reference point when centering the lens; when the stylus is centered on the field guide, the lens is centered on the compound. And when the north/south and east/west cranks are turned to move the compound, the stylus also moves to indicate the movement on the field guide. The pantograph is a convenient device for locating and planning camera movement.

One feature common to all animation stand camera setups is the **frame counter.** The most advanced stands have electronic rather than mechanical counters, but both are suitable. A frame counter tells you how many frames are exposed and is a double check to make sure that the animator is at the correct point on the exposure sheet.

The type of **viewfinder** used in animation is the reflex type, which enables the operator to see an image formed directly by the lens to ensure proper field coverage. Many large stands also have rack-over viewfinders which make it possible for the operator to line up the shot without a

THE OXBERRY 5442C Master Series Animation Stand—The state of the art. You are looking at an on-line computer controlled animation system capable of 16 mm or 35 mm filming. It permits precision computer control over the entire operation of the stand. The operator can direct the computer to execute complex sequences of animation photography with simple instructions in "animation language." The computer console is on the left and the aerial image projection unit is on the lower right.

reflex viewfinder. In either case, each scene must be properly aligned with the lens.

In basic mechanical setups, the lens should be focused or checked for focus after each frame in a zoom shot. The large automated stands have automatic follow-focus cams connected to the lens by a gearing system that moves the focus ring as the camera moves up and down the vertical column. There is a different cam for each different lens and the cams must be changed when the lenses are changed.

In-camera fades and dissolves

can easily be done by closing the shutter down frame by frame for the number of frames desired in the effect. Again, while fades and dissolves can be done manually, they are usually performed automatically on the more sophisticated animation stand cameras. In-camera dissolves, of course, save on the budget since the scene transition does not have to be created later in the lab. The large animation stands have **control consoles** which allow the operator to preselect much of the camera's shutter action. Basic controls usually include a motor switch or main switch for the power supply, a forward/reverse switch, a camera speed selector, a single-frame button, fade/dissolve selector, speed rheostat, and many other controls. The computerized stands of today also have automated controls for the compound movement in east-west or north-south modes or combinations.

When you're ready to film, there are a few **lighting** tips you should be familiar with. For most work within a 12-field area you only need two light sources. The area to be lit is determined by the widest field size that can be photographed. Place each light on either side of the compound at a 45-degree angle to eliminate

reflections. Then, hold an incident light meter near the platen, directly under the lens, to check the light level prior to shooting. Also, check the lamps to make sure that they have an equal light output, and move the meter over the largest field area to be used, adjusting light angles and distances so the illumination is even.

As in all photography, the smaller the f/stop the greater the depth of field, so keeping an appropriate f/stop will control the near-to-far distance over which the image will be sharp. This is particularly important when filming three-dimensional objects or puppets. As you know, if the f/stop is a small diameter, the lens opening will also be small, which means you may need more lighting on the artwork for the same length of exposure. Try higher-wattage lamps, but make sure you don't overload your electrical circuits. Also, be sure to use lamps of the proper color temperature for the film or films and filter combinations you use.

To minimize glare and reflection from the light, use **polarizing filters**, such as KODAK POLASCREENS, on both the lights and the lens. But make sure that the polarizing filters on the lamps are not too close to the bulbs because they are usually made of a plastic material that will not tolerate excess heat. The best way to check the alignment of the polarizing filters is to set up the filters and place a small, very shiny silver coin in the center of the field guide directly under the lens.

Then, turn on one light only, and revolve the screen in front of it so that the axis (as indicated by the arrow on the polarizing screen) is horizontal. If the camera has through-the-lens viewing (reflex or ground glass), put the polarizing filter in place over the camera lens and rotate it until the reflec-

tions from the coin, seen through the filter and camera lens, are at a minimum.

If the arrow on the filter at the light is horizontal, as suggested above, any indicating arrow or handle on the camera polarizing filter will usually be vertical or rotated 90 degrees from the arrow.

Now, turn out the first light and turn on the second light. Then, without disturbing the setting of the filter on the camera lens, rotate the screen in front of the second light until the reflections from the coin, as seen through the reflex viewfinder of the camera (or the filter at the camera), are again at a minimum. When you make this last adjustment, the lighting setup will be adjusted for minimum surface reflection.

Don't forget that you need to adjust the exposure when art is illuminated by polarized light and photographed through a polarizing filter. To determine the correct exposure, take an incident-light meter reading of the art with the polarizing screens over the copy lights. Increase the indicated exposure by opening the diaphragm 1⅓ stops more than the meter reading.

This will compensate for the polarizing filter over the camera lens. Using this exposure as a starting point, you should make about four more exposures to determine what setting is best for your particular copy situation: ½ stop over, 1 stop over, ½ stop under, and 1 stop under.

You might want to record the best exposure setting, as well as any other relevant information, for future reference in similar situations.

PART FOUR

Building Your Own Animation Stand

Index

This part contains all the instructions you need to build your own working animation stand. The approximate construction time is 85 hours, including cutting time. Most of the items are available through any well-equipped hardware store, and you can buy the acrylic sheets through a plastic sheeting distributor (see your Yellow Pages). The PVC plastic pipe and fittings should be available at any plumbing supply store. The animation stand we built is fitted with an animation disc that has an Oxberry registration system. You can order the disc from Oxberry Division (Richmark Camera Service, Inc.), 180-T Broad Street, Carlstadt, New Jersey 07072, (201) 935-3000. If Acme registration is standard in your area (mostly in the western U.S.), Acme as well as Oxberry distributors can be found by calling your nearest camera and cinema equipment supply house. Animators in Europe and other parts of the world should check with existing animation studios for the standard cel registration system. The animation disc is optional and allows for spins and some cel and background travel. However, if you don't need a stand with the versatility the disc offers, you can buy a simple registration peg bar that you can tape down. The tape-down peg bars are also available through your nearest camera equipment supply house.

This build-it-yourself animation stand will accommodate a lightweight 16 mm or super 8 camera stand and has a compound capable of north-south and east-west movements on a horizontal plane, and in-and-out zooms on a vertical plane. If you purchase the disc, you will have the added capability of traveling peg bars and a spinning disc. The stand is basic, but has good capability for complex camera work. You can also make your own modifications to suit your individual needs.

PARTS LIST*

Here's a shopping list for all the materials you need to build your stand. We have also shown all the finished pieces in the photo on the right. Follow pages 64-69 to cut your pieces. Then, use the plans on pages 70-72 to align your wooden parts, and follow the more detailed steps starting on page 73.

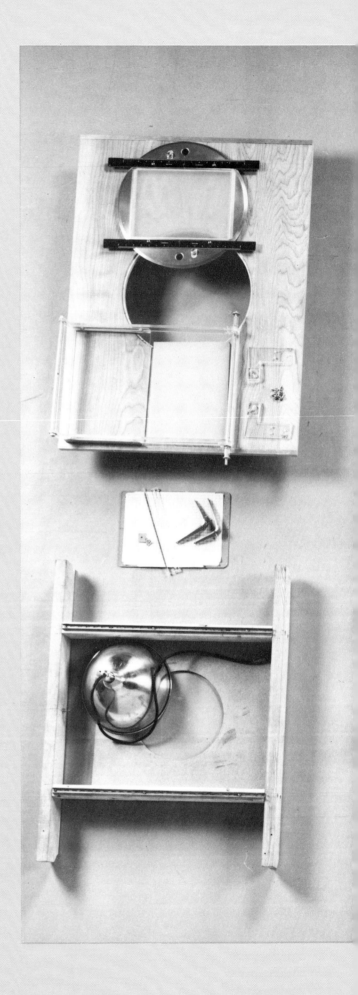

1. eight 8-ft 2 x 4-in planks	$ 16.00
2. one 4-ft 2 x 3-in plank	5.00
3. six 2-ft 4 x 4-in planks	10.00
4. Sheet birch plywood—¾ in x 31 in x 42 in	16.00
5. 6-ft x ¾-in aluminum channel	4.50
6. 2-ft x 1-in right-angle aluminum edge molding	1.85
7. four 6-ft metal wall bracket tracks @ 3.17 ea	12.68
8. four 8-in strap hinges with ⅜-in pin openings (pin openings may have to be reamed to size)	5.98
9. three 36-in x ⅜-in threaded steel rods and ⅜-in nuts	4.80
10. two casement-type window crank handles @ 1.39 ea	2.80
11. two 10-ft x 4-in PVC sewer pipe	10.00
12. four 4-ft PVC couplings (for camera mount)	4.00
13. two 4-in PVC "T" connectors	4.00
14. four 4-in PVC end caps	4.00
15. 6-ft x ⅜-in (interior diameter) plastic tubing	2.70
16. (a) piece of ⅜-in acrylic sheeting 12 in x 24 in	4.50
(b) piece of ¼-in acrylic sheeting 24 in x 48 in	12.00
(c) piece of rubber pad 5 in x 3½ in	.50
17. piece 10-in x 15 in x ¼-in plate glass (obtain optical-quality-glass if possible, for platen)	5.00
18. four 4½-in diameter hose clamps	2.36
19. two telescoping tripod light stands	20.00
20. (a) clamp-on light sockets	6.00
(b) two 10-in reflectors	6.00
(c) one 12-in reflector	4.00
21. (a) one electrical extension cord with four sockets	8.00
(b) one junction box with two switches and two receptacles	6.50
(c) two 9-ft extension cords	2.14
22. (a) eight 5-in carriage bolts (¼ in)	1.20
(b) twenty-eight 3-in lag screws (¼ in)	4.20
(c) forty-eight 2½-in lag screws (¼ in)	4.80
(d) four ⅜-in x 3-in machine bolts and nuts	1.10
(e) one hundred ¼-in flat washers	1.20
(f) two ¾-in hose clamps	.98
(g) eight 3-in #10 wood screws	.85
(h) twelve ⅛-in x 1-in stove bolts	.69
(i) thirty-four 1-in #6 round head wood screws	1.00
(j) two ¼-in x 16-in wing nuts (camera mount)	.49
(k) one ¼-in x 1-in x 16-in carriage bolt	.15
(l) one ¼-in x 3-in eye bolt	.15
(m) four 1-in #10 sheet metal screws	.20
(n) eight ¾-in #6 round head wood screws	.35
(o) one steel pipe bracket	.35
23. one roll strapping iron	1.49
24. one 10-in x 14-in x ¼-in foam pad (for platen)	.10
25. one tube wheel bearing grease (available at bicycle or auto parts stores)	2.50
26. (a) two pieces of ¼-in Masonite board (22 in x 23 in, 11 in x 14 in)	1.50
(b) one Oxberry field guide (for pantograph)	4.00
(c) one ¼-in plastic rod (10 in long) for stylus on pantograph	.45
(d) two 4-in x 6-in rectangle shelf brackets	1.29
27. one can PVC cement, 8 oz (not shown)	1.89
28. one bottle acrylic cement, 6 oz (not shown)	.85
29. one tape-down peg bar (not shown)	20.00
TOTAL PART COST	**$233.19**

NOTE: Add approximately $180 if you choose to purchase the Oxberry disc.

*Prices based on 1978 figures.

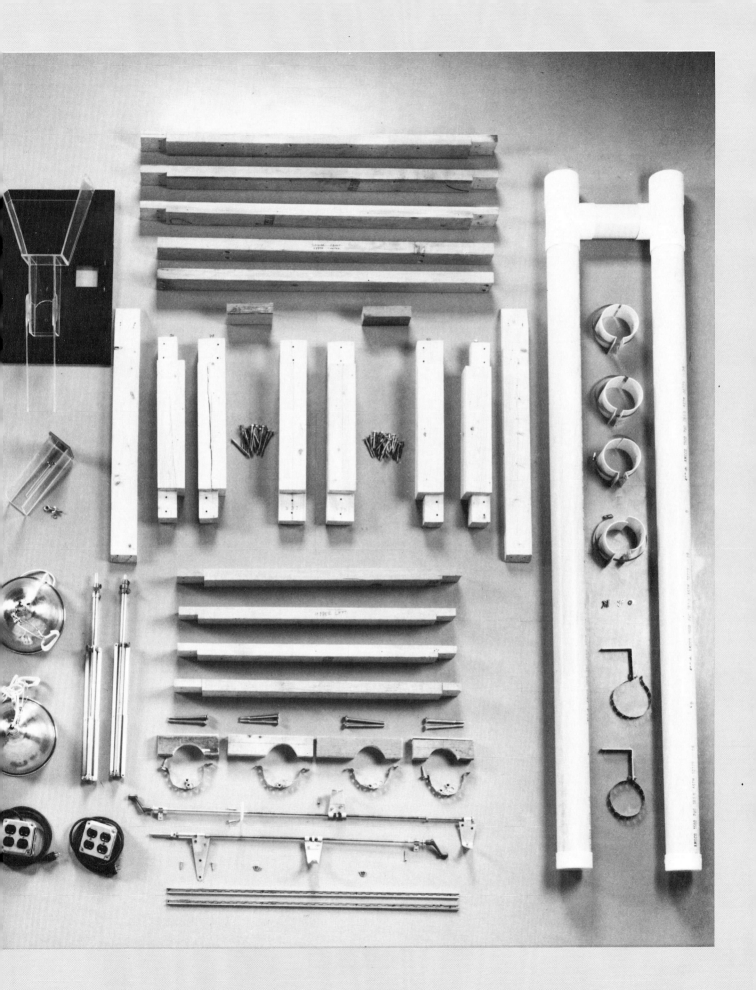

WOOD PIECES
BASE PARTS

POSTS FROM 6 - 24" 4×4'S (ACTUAL $3\frac{1}{2}$" × $3\frac{1}{2}$")

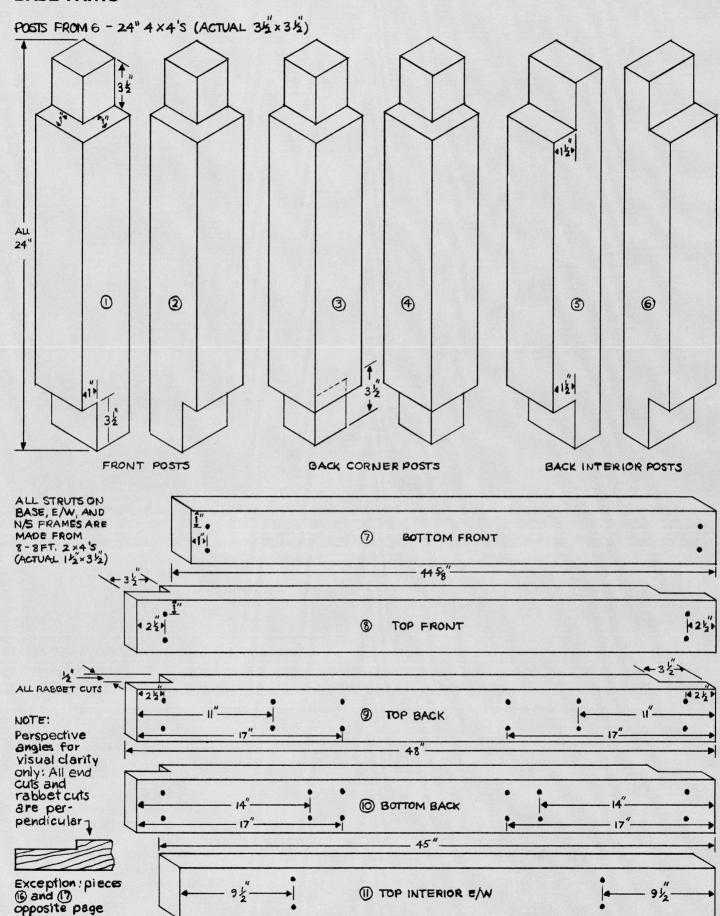

FRONT POSTS   BACK CORNER POSTS   BACK INTERIOR POSTS

ALL STRUTS ON BASE, E/W, AND N/S FRAMES ARE MADE FROM 8 - 8 FT. 2×4'S (ACTUAL $1\frac{1}{2}$" × $3\frac{1}{2}$")

⑦ BOTTOM FRONT

⑧ TOP FRONT

ALL RABBET CUTS

NOTE:
Perspective angles for visual clarity only: All end cuts and rabbet cuts are perpendicular

⑨ TOP BACK

⑩ BOTTOM BACK

⑪ TOP INTERIOR E/W

Exception: pieces ⑯ and ⑰ opposite page

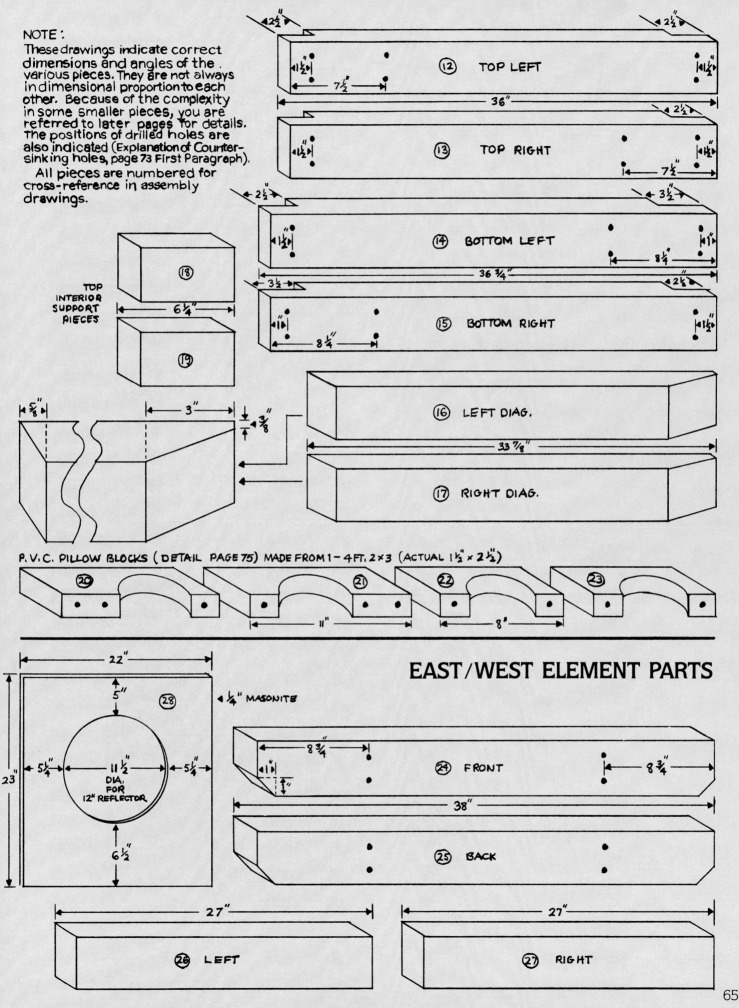

NOTE:
These drawings indicate correct dimensions and angles of the various pieces. They are not always in dimensional proportion to each other. Because of the complexity in some smaller pieces, you are referred to later pages for details. The positions of drilled holes are also indicated (Explanation of Counter-sinking holes, page 73 First Paragraph).

All pieces are numbered for cross-reference in assembly drawings.

(12) TOP LEFT

(13) TOP RIGHT

(14) BOTTOM LEFT

(15) BOTTOM RIGHT

(16) LEFT DIAG.

(17) RIGHT DIAG.

(18)
(19)
TOP INTERIOR SUPPORT PIECES

P.V.C. PILLOW BLOCKS (DETAIL PAGE 75) MADE FROM 1-4 FT. 2×3 (ACTUAL 1½" × 2½")

(20) (21) (22) (23)

EAST/WEST ELEMENT PARTS

(28)
¼" MASONITE
11½" DIA. FOR 12" REFLECTOR

(24) FRONT

(25) BACK

(26) LEFT

(27) RIGHT

WOOD PIECES

NORTH/SOUTH ELEMENT PARTS

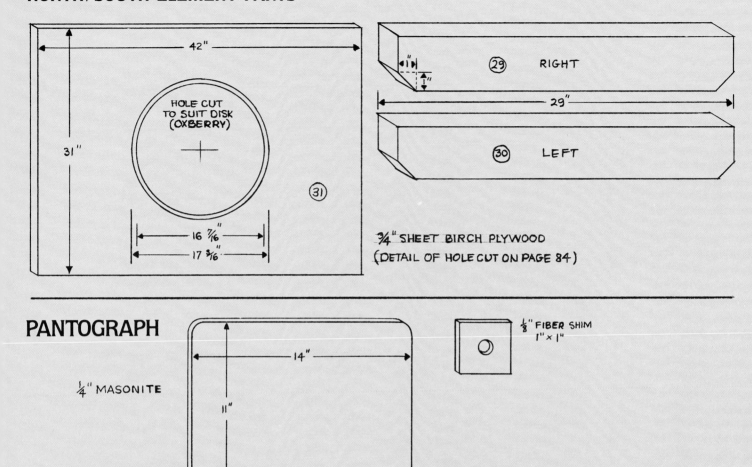

42"

31"

HOLE CUT
TO SUIT DISK
(OXBERRY)

31

16 7/16"

17 3/16"

1"

1"

29 RIGHT

29"

30 LEFT

3/4" SHEET BIRCH PLYWOOD
(DETAIL OF HOLE CUT ON PAGE 84)

PANTOGRAPH

1/4" MASONITE

14"

11"

1" ROUNDED CORNERS

1/8" FIBER SHIM
1" × 1"

PVC PIECES

ALL CUT PIECES FROM 2 - 10 FT. × 4 IN. PVC SEWER PIPE

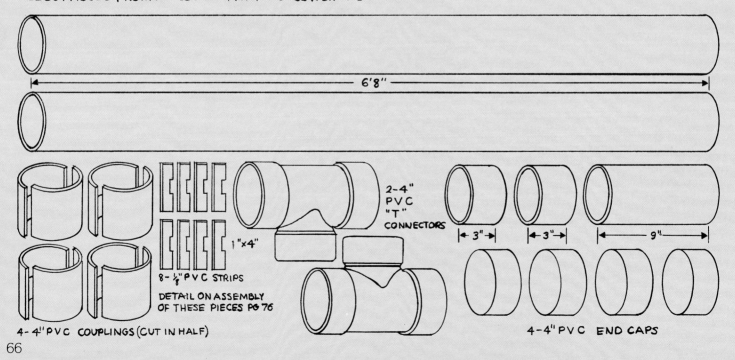

6'8"

2-4"
PVC
"T"
CONNECTORS

1"×4"

8 - 1/8" PVC STRIPS

DETAIL ON ASSEMBLY
OF THESE PIECES PG 76

4-4" PVC COUPLINGS (CUT IN HALF)

3"

3"

9"

4-4" PVC END CAPS

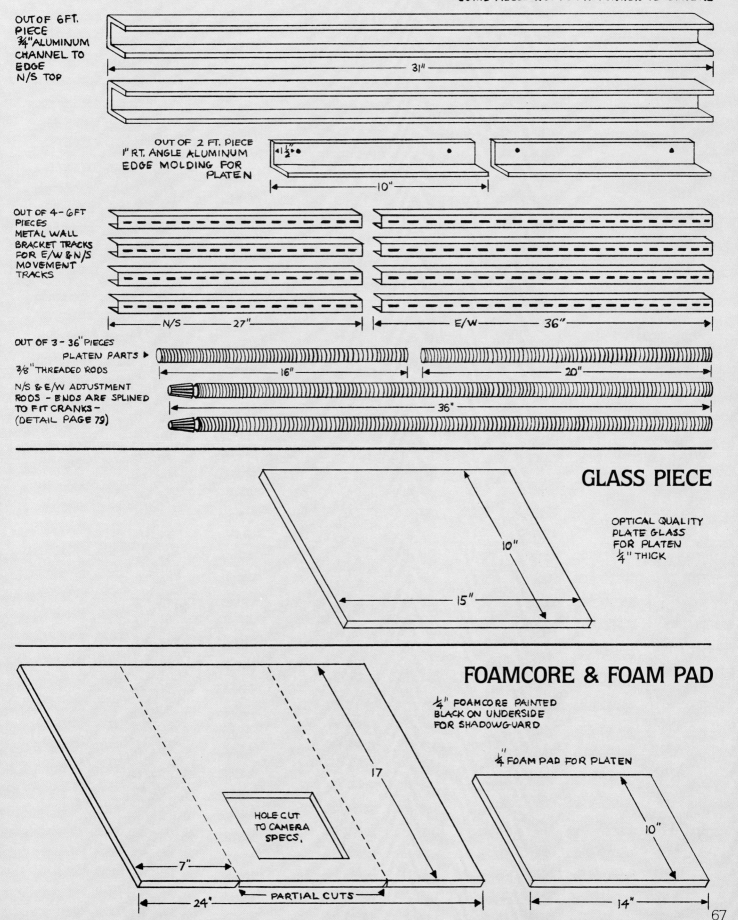

METAL PIECES

(INCLUDES ONLY CUT PIECES - NOT STANDARD HARDWARE)
SOME PIECES NOT IN PROPORTION TO OTHERS

OUT OF 6 FT.
PIECE
3/4" ALUMINUM
CHANNEL TO
EDGE
N/S TOP

31"

OUT OF 2 FT. PIECE
1" RT. ANGLE ALUMINUM
EDGE MOLDING FOR
PLATEN

1 1/2"

10"

OUT OF 4 - 6FT
PIECES
METAL WALL
BRACKET TRACKS
FOR E/W & N/S
MOVEMENT
TRACKS

N/S   27"

E/W   36"

OUT OF 3 - 36" PIECES
PLATEN PARTS ▶

3/8" THREADED RODS

16"

20"

N/S & E/W ADJUSTMENT
RODS - ENDS ARE SPLINED
TO FIT CRANKS -
(DETAIL PAGE 79)

36"

GLASS PIECE

OPTICAL QUALITY
PLATE GLASS
FOR PLATEN
1/4" THICK

10"

15"

FOAMCORE & FOAM PAD

1/4" FOAMCORE PAINTED
BLACK ON UNDERSIDE
FOR SHADOWGUARD

1/4" FOAM PAD FOR PLATEN

17"

HOLE CUT
TO CAMERA
SPECS.

10"

7"

PARTIAL CUTS

24"

14"

ACRYLIC PIECES

3/8" TUBING

(INTERIOR DIMENSION)
(OUT OF 6 FT. PIECE

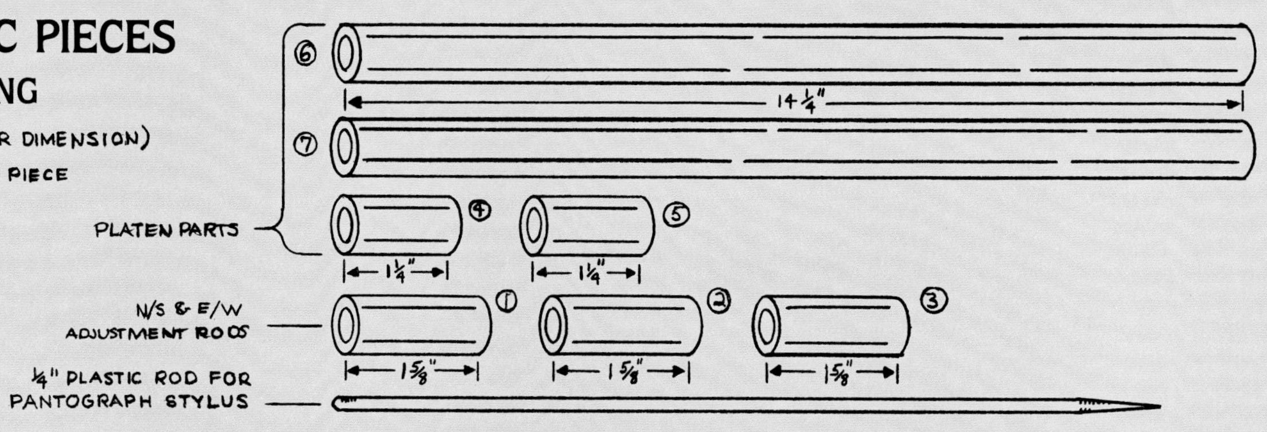

⑥
⑦
14 1/4"
PLATEN PARTS
④
⑤
1 1/4"
1 1/4"
N/S & E/W ADJUSTMENT RODS
①
②
③
1 5/8"
1 5/8"
1 5/8"
1/4" PLASTIC ROD FOR PANTOGRAPH STYLUS

3/8" ACRYLIC PIECES (TWO OF THESE PIECES ARE THE ONLY 3/8" PIECES IN THE ENTIRE STAND.)

OUT OF 12"x24" SHEET

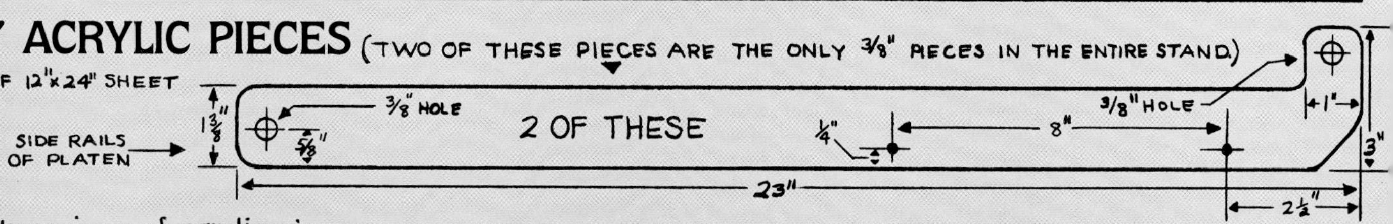

SIDE RAILS OF PLATEN
1 3/8"
3/8" HOLE
5/8"
2 OF THESE
1/4"
8"
3/8" HOLE
1"
3"
23"
2 1/2"

All dimensions of acrylic pieces are finished dimensions.

Perspective edges are used in this section to illustrate ONLY the edges which are NOT perpendicular cuts.

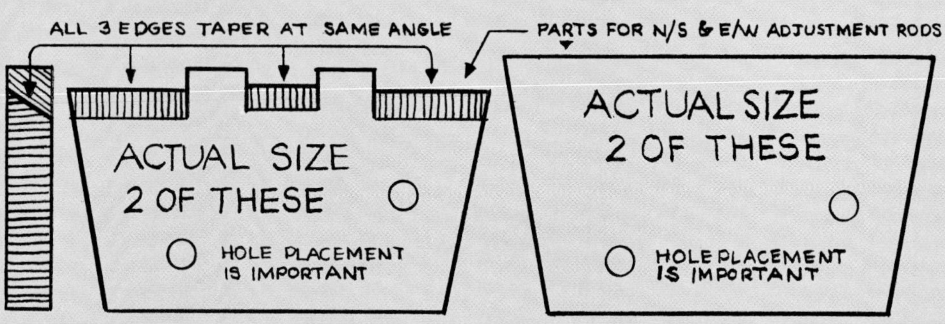

ALL 3 EDGES TAPER AT SAME ANGLE
PARTS FOR N/S & E/W ADJUSTMENT RODS
ACTUAL SIZE
2 OF THESE
HOLE PLACEMENT IS IMPORTANT
ACTUAL SIZE
2 OF THESE
HOLE PLACEMENT IS IMPORTANT

1/4" ACRYLIC PIECES ▶

OUT OF 24"x48" SHEET

From this point, all of these drawings and those on the opposing page are in dimensional proportion to each other. Scale 3/8" = 1"

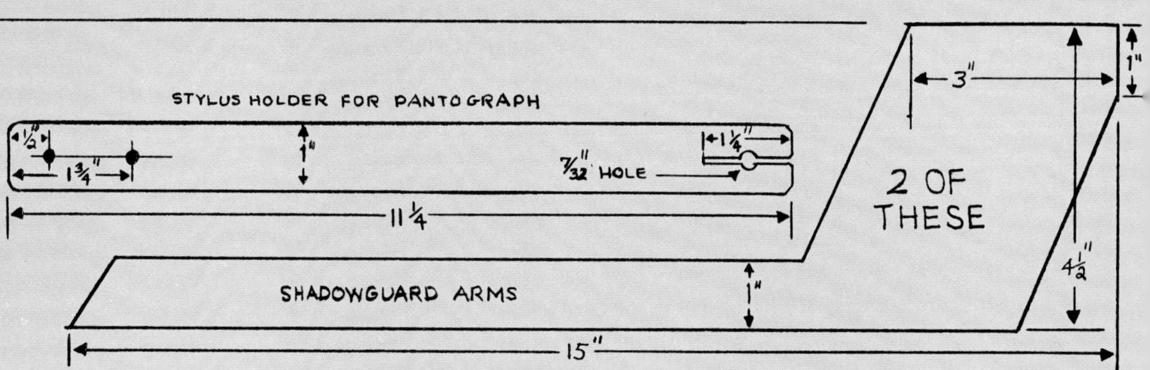

STYLUS HOLDER FOR PANTOGRAPH
1/2"
1 3/4"
1"
1 1/4"
7/32" HOLE
11 1/4
3"
1"
2 OF THESE
4 1/2"
SHADOWGUARD ARMS
1"
15"

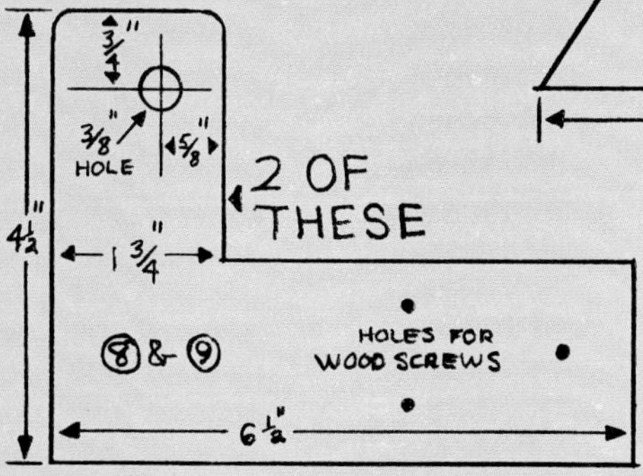

3/4"
3/8" HOLE
5/8"
2 OF THESE
4 1/2"
1 3/4"
⑧ & ⑨
HOLES FOR WOOD SCREWS
6 1/2"
2"

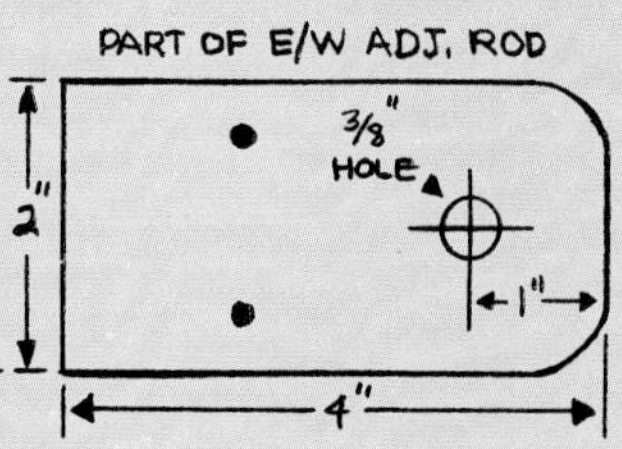

PART OF E/W ADJ. ROD
3/8" HOLE
1"
4"

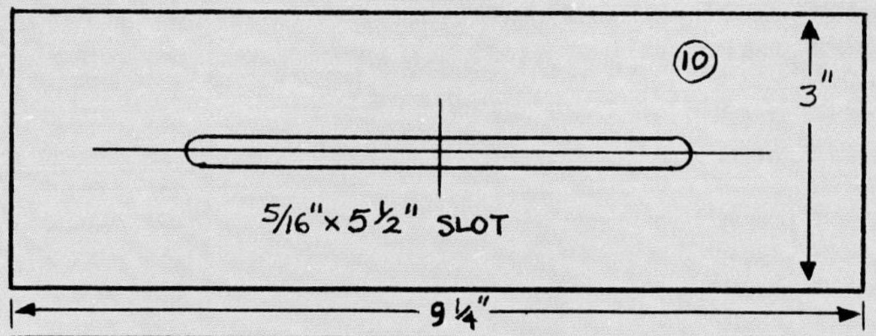

⑩
3"
5/16" x 5 1/2" SLOT
9 1/4"

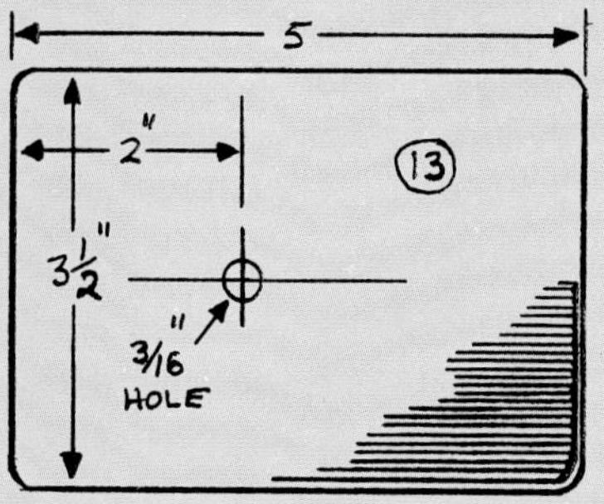

5
2"
⑬
3 1/2"
3/16" HOLE

Camera Pad is faced with a section of rubber mat to cushion tightening of camera

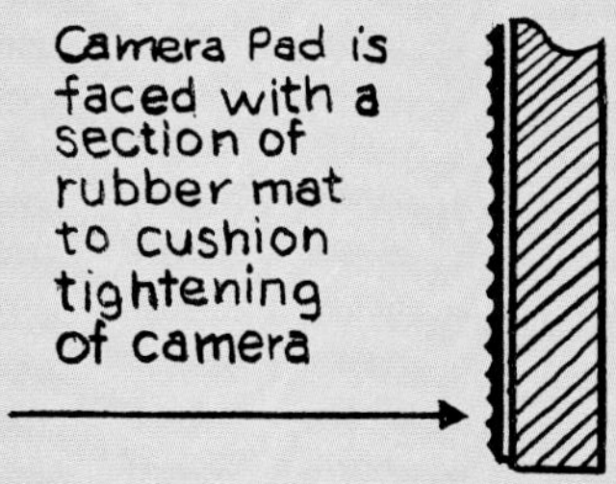

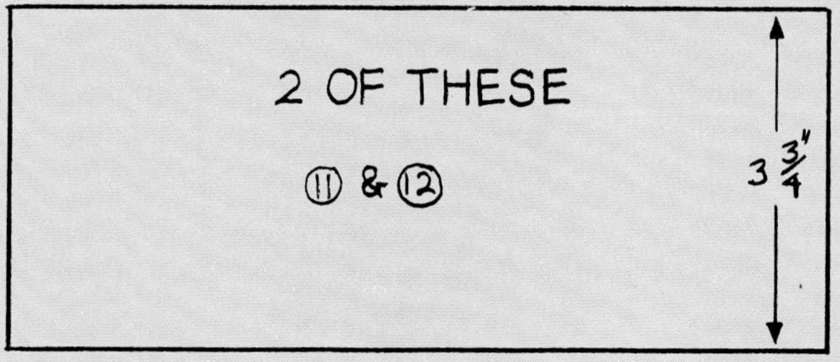

2 OF THESE
⑪ & ⑫
3 3/4"

¼" ACRYLIC PIECES

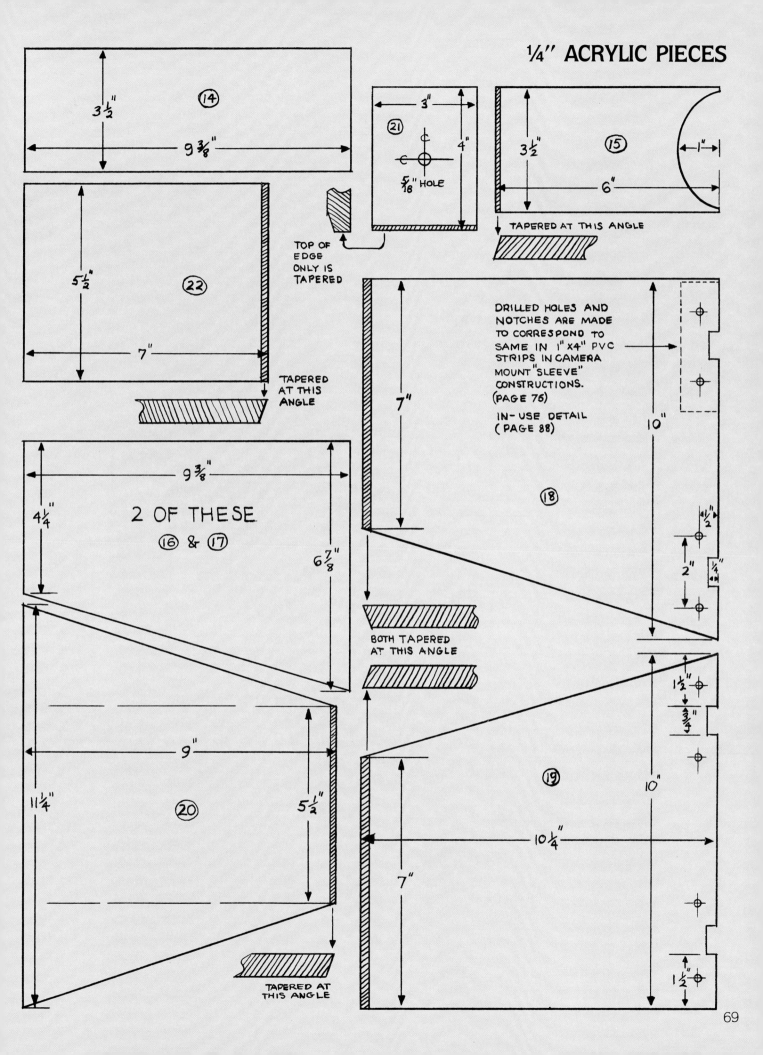

⑭ 3½" 9⅜"

⑳ 3" 4" ⅝" HOLE

TOP OF EDGE ONLY IS TAPERED

⑮ 3½" 6" 1"

TAPERED AT THIS ANGLE

㉒ 5½" 7"

TAPERED AT THIS ANGLE

DRILLED HOLES AND NOTCHES ARE MADE TO CORRESPOND TO SAME IN 1"X4" PVC STRIPS IN CAMERA MOUNT "SLEEVE" CONSTRUCTIONS. (PAGE 75)

IN-USE DETAIL (PAGE 88)

2 OF THESE ⑯ & ⑰

9⅜" 4¼" 6⅞"

⑱ 7" 10" 4½" 2" ¼"

BOTH TAPERED AT THIS ANGLE

⑳ 9" 11¼" 5½"

⑲ 1½" ¾" 10" 10¼" 7" 1½"

TAPERED AT THIS ANGLE

69

BASE CONSTRUCTION
(FRONT VIEW)

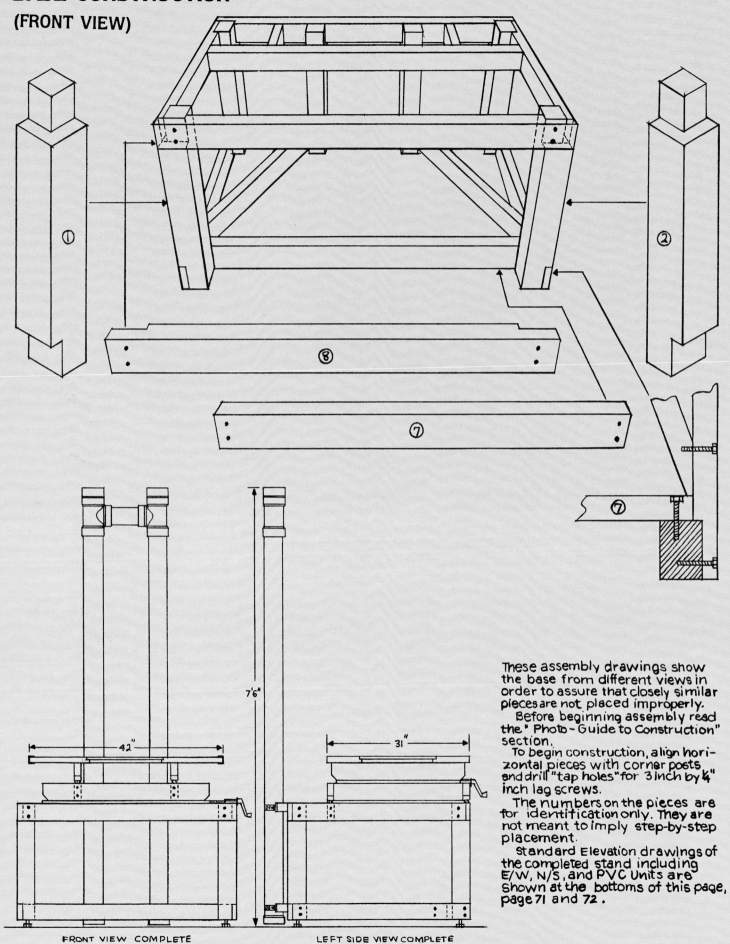

These assembly drawings show the base from different views in order to assure that closely similar pieces are not placed improperly.

Before beginning assembly read the "Photo-Guide to Construction" section.

To begin construction, align horizontal pieces with corner posts and drill "tap holes" for 3 inch by ¼" inch lag screws.

The numbers on the pieces are for identification only. They are not meant to imply step-by-step placement.

Standard Elevation drawings of the completed stand including E/W, N/S, and PVC Units are shown at the bottoms of this page, page 71 and 72.

FRONT VIEW COMPLETE

LEFT SIDE VIEW COMPLETE

BASE CONSTRUCTION
(¾ FRONT VIEW)

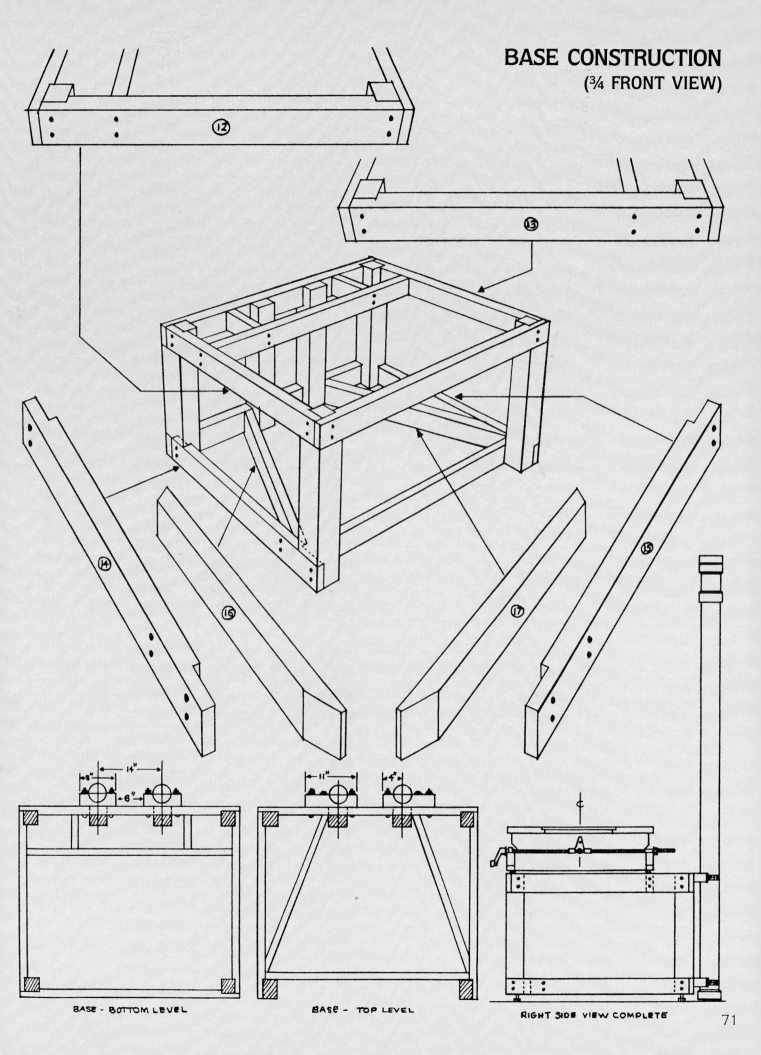

⑫

⑬

⑭

⑮

⑯

⑰

BASE - BOTTOM LEVEL

BASE - TOP LEVEL

RIGHT SIDE VIEW COMPLETE

BASE CONSTRUCTION
(BACK VIEW)

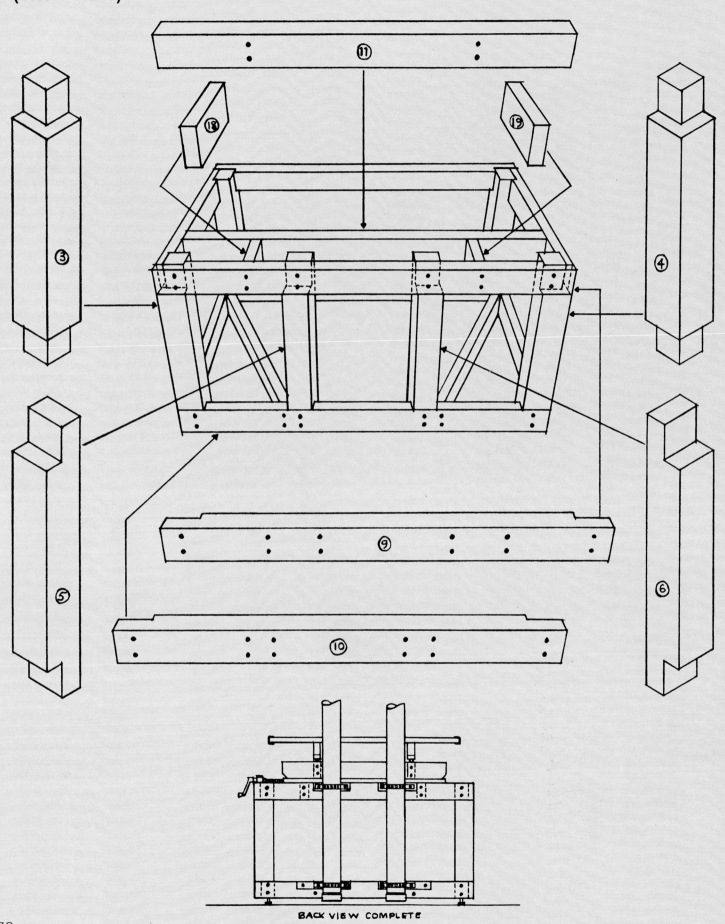

BACK VIEW COMPLETE

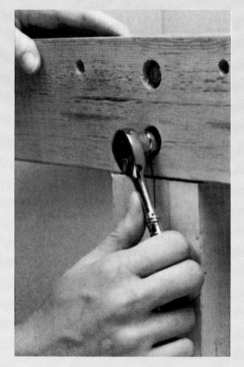

After the wood is cut to the dimensions shown in the drawn plan, drill out all the rabbet-cut ends as shown with a ¼-inch drill bit about 1¼ inches from the edge and 2½ inches from the ends. Prior to assembly, sand the rough edges with a medium-grade sandpaper to eliminate splinters and the rough finish. Use ¾-inch wood boring bit for countersinking all the holes. The washers can be set into the holes ahead of time for faster assembly.

The corners with rabbet-cut ends are fixed with the 2½-inch by ¼-inch lag screws. Do not tighten them at this point. Use the 2½-inch screws for the front part of the angle braces, too. Fasten all other pieces with the 3-inch by ¼-inch lag screws.

Use a Spin-Tite or ratchet to set the lag screws. Be careful not to tighten them at this point, so that the base can be slipped into place prior to final tightening.

Insert the screws in the holes drilled to meet the angle braces at their thickest point.

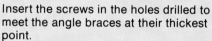

If the wood is soft, do not drill tap holes in the braces. Tighten just enough for the base to hold together.

After you complete the base, mount the junction box with switches as shown on the upper front, right side of the base.

Note the detail on the two-switch electrical junction box. It is fitted with two combination switch/outlet receptacles and wired so that the switch operates the outlet.

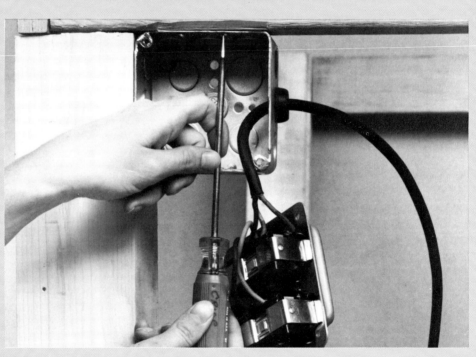

When assembly is complete, stand the frame upright on a very flat, even surface and tighten all the screws.

Fasten the 36-inch tracks as shown. Center the tracks from left to right and make them flush with the inside edges.

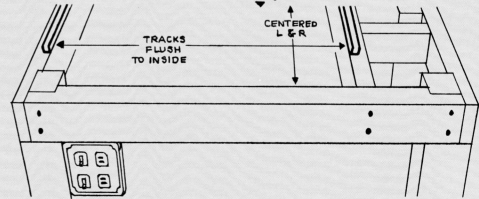

CENTERED
L & R

TRACKS
FLUSH
TO INSIDE

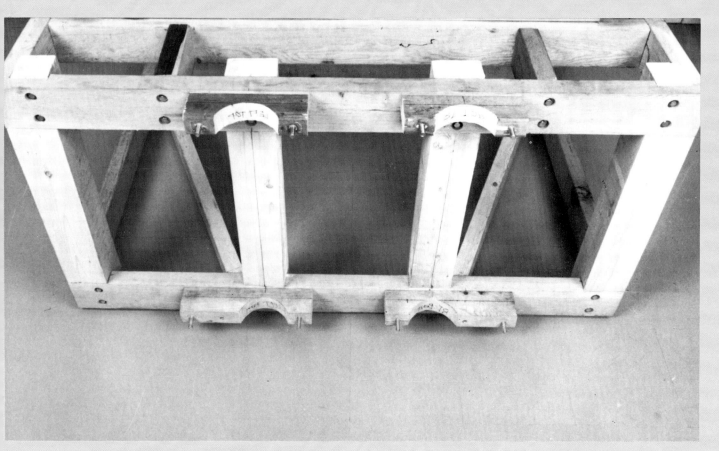

Now assemble the pillow blocks to the upper- and lower-rear crossmembers with 5-inch carriage bolts. The block centers should be 14 inches apart.

Insert the bolts from inside the structure; do not use the nuts now, they will be used later to anchor the PVC pipe with the banding irons.

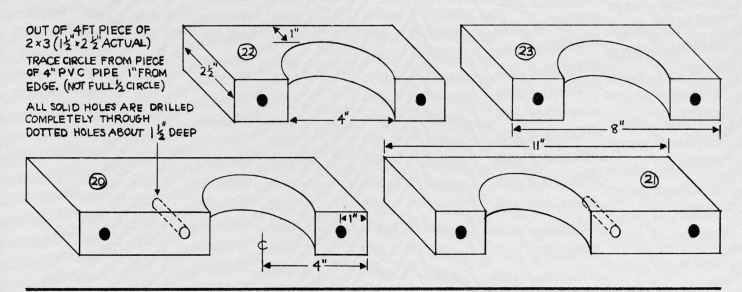

OUT OF 4FT PIECE OF
2×3 (1½"×2½" ACTUAL)

TRACE CIRCLE FROM PIECE OF 4" PVC PIPE 1" FROM EDGE. (NOT FULL ½ CIRCLE)

ALL SOLID HOLES ARE DRILLED COMPLETELY THROUGH
DOTTED HOLES ABOUT 1½" DEEP

NOTE:
At this point (before further modules are added to the structure) provision should be made for leveling the finished stand. Turn the base on its side and sink ⅜" × 3-inch machine nuts and bolts into ⅜-inch holes drilled into corners of the base.(Photo page 81).

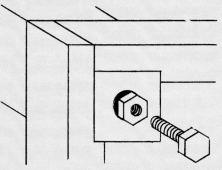

PVC STRUCTURE ASSEMBLY

Before gluing PVC structure together with PVC Glue, test-fit all pieces. It is important that the resulting structure be exactly 14" wide on centers of posts. It must match pillow blocks on base.

CAMERA MOUNT SLEEVE CONSTRUCTION

Cut 4 - 4" PVC Couplings in half and remove the inside ridge with a rasp or grinding wheel. Cut 8 - 1" x 4" PVC strips($\frac{1}{8}$") and notch for hose-clamps. Cement strips on inside cut edges of couplings. Be sure that notch is deep enough so that clamps can pass easily after gluing.

Position finished sleeves towards top of structure.

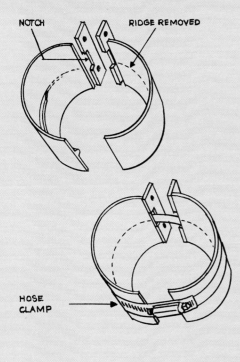

NOTCH   RIDGE REMOVED

HOSE CLAMP

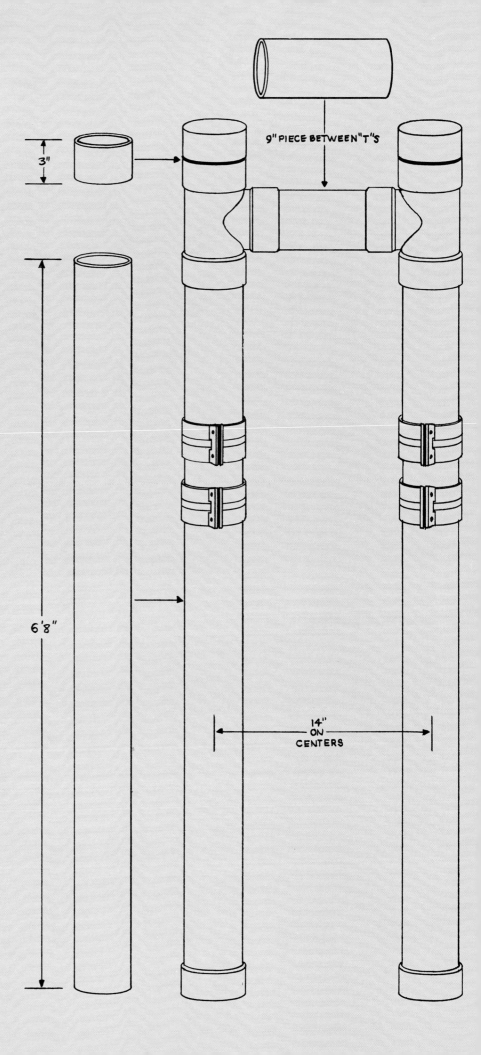

3"

9" PIECE BETWEEN "T"S

6'8"

14"
ON
CENTERS

The assembled vertical PVC pipes are fixed to the pillow blocks with the perforated banding irons and the nuts for the carriage bolts. Be sure the PVC pipes are firm. If the wood is soft, be careful not to overtighten bolts.

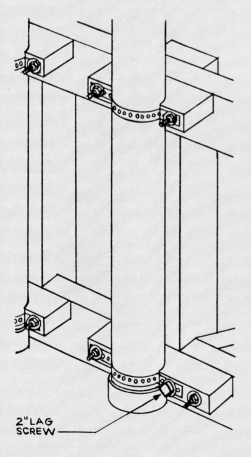

2" LAG SCREW

The lower band is fixed on the inside to the 5-inch carriage bolt and on the outside with a 2-inch lag screw with flat washers. Insert a small shim underneath to allow for clearance in vertical adjustments of the stand.

EAST/WEST FRAME ASSEMBLY
(FRONT VIEW)

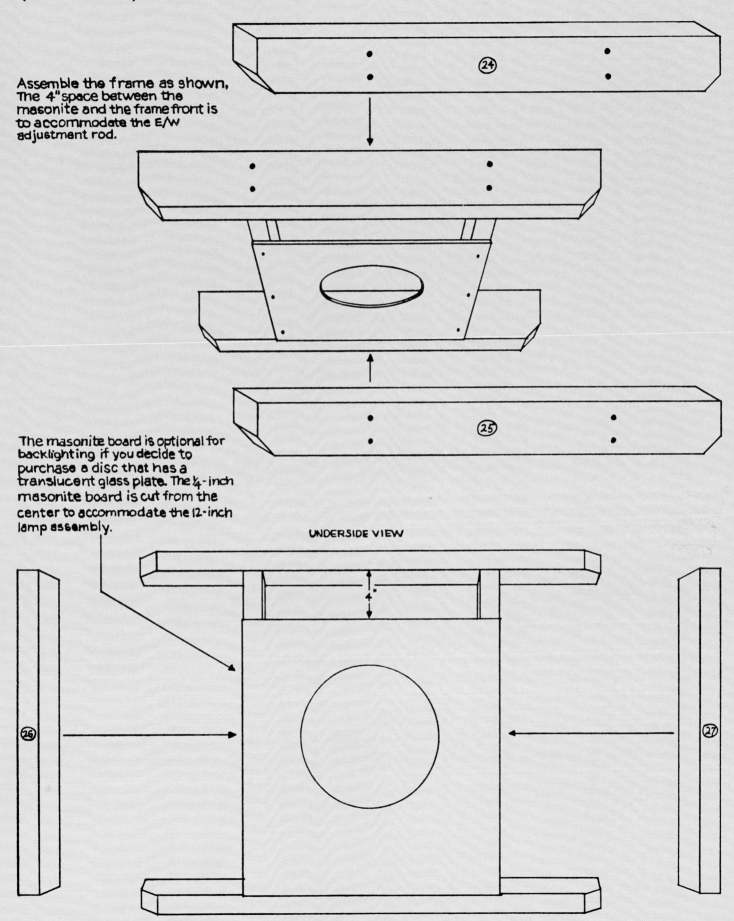

Assemble the frame as shown. The 4" space between the masonite and the frame front is to accommodate the E/W adjustment rod.

The masonite board is optional for backlighting if you decide to purchase a disc that has a translucent glass plate. The 1/4-inch masonite board is cut from the center to accommodate the 12-inch lamp assembly.

UNDERSIDE VIEW

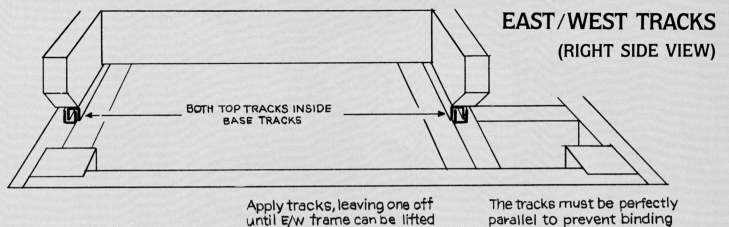

EAST/WEST TRACKS
(RIGHT SIDE VIEW)

BOTH TOP TRACKS INSIDE BASE TRACKS

Apply tracks, leaving one off until E/W frame can be lifted onto base, for final track placement.

The tracks must be perfectly parallel to prevent binding and to assure smooth motion.

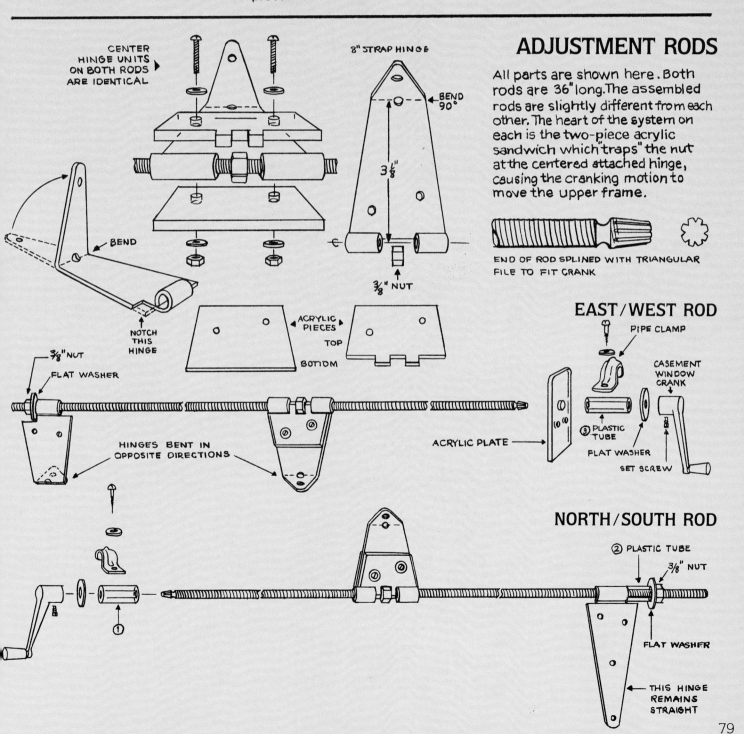

ADJUSTMENT RODS

All parts are shown here. Both rods are 36" long. The assembled rods are slightly different from each other. The heart of the system on each is the two-piece acrylic sandwich which "traps" the nut at the centered attached hinge, causing the cranking motion to move the upper frame.

CENTER HINGE UNITS ON BOTH RODS ARE IDENTICAL

8" STRAP HINGE

BEND 90°

$3\frac{1}{8}$"

$\frac{3}{8}$" NUT

BEND

NOTCH THIS HINGE

ACRYLIC PIECES
TOP
BOTTOM

END OF ROD SPLINED WITH TRIANGULAR FILE TO FIT CRANK

EAST/WEST ROD

PIPE CLAMP

CASEMENT WINDOW CRANK

③ PLASTIC TUBE

FLAT WASHER

SET SCREW

ACRYLIC PLATE

$\frac{3}{8}$" NUT

FLAT WASHER

HINGES BENT IN OPPOSITE DIRECTIONS

NORTH/SOUTH ROD

①

② PLASTIC TUBE

$\frac{3}{8}$" NUT

FLAT WASHER

THIS HINGE REMAINS STRAIGHT

EAST/WEST FRAME ATTACHMENT

The east-west movement is fixed to the frame using a ¼-inch acrylic plate. (See drawn plan)

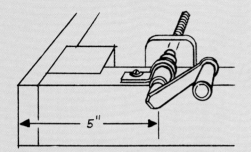

Using the ⅜-inch I.D. (interior diameter) plastic tube for a bushing, cut a section out as described in the drawing, and clamp it down with a steel pipe bracket, with the plastic tube flush with the plate. NOTE: Use a piece of tape to hold up the other end for now.

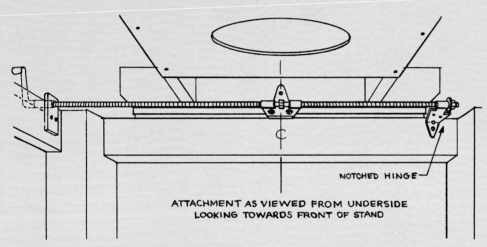

ATTACHMENT AS VIEWED FROM UNDERSIDE LOOKING TOWARDS FRONT OF STAND

NOTCHED HINGE

The east-west frame is fitted onto the ½-inch steel channel tracks after wheel bearing grease (shown on page 81) is applied to the channels.

Rub wheel bearing grease on the movement channels.

Crank the east-west control bracket to the center and attach the hinge mount to the center line with a 1½-inch x 10-inch panhead metal screw (as shown in drawing on the opposite page).

After lubricating the channel, mount it so that the upper tracks overlap on the inside to prevent shifting, as previously detailed.

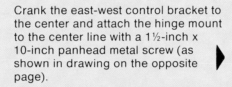

Crank the east-west control bracket to the center and attach the hinge mount to the center line with a 1½-inch x 10-inch panhead metal screw (as shown in drawing on the opposite page).

Center and fasten the 27-inch metal tracks on top of the side rails of E/W frame in preparation for N/S frame mounting. Tracks are also shown in photo to right.

Move the east-west frame to center over the base and mark a perpendicular center line on both pieces of wood for future alignment.

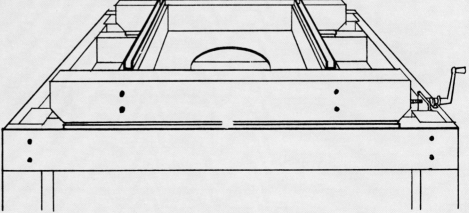

NORTH/SOUTH
FRAME ASSEMBLY

Attach ¾" aluminum channel to sides of birch plywood to give top "drawing board" accuracy in relation to animation disk.

Support members ㉙ and ㉚ are glued to top. Make sure they are parallel.

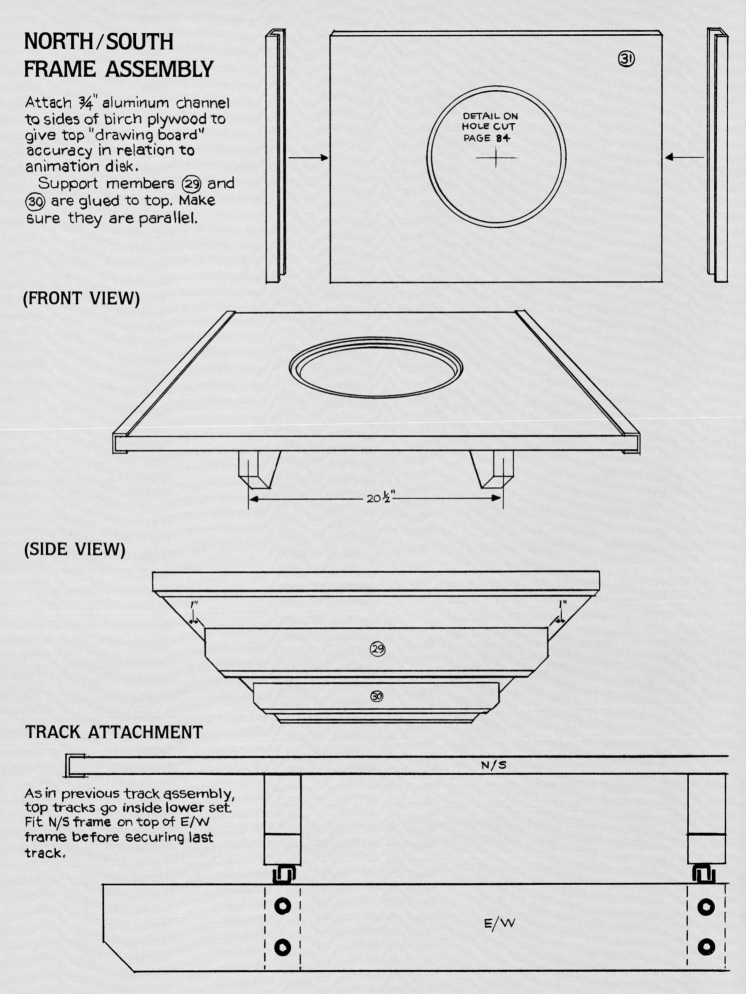

(FRONT VIEW)

DETAIL ON HOLE CUT PAGE 84

㉛

20½"

(SIDE VIEW)

1"   1"

㉙

㉚

TRACK ATTACHMENT

N/S

As in previous track assembly, top tracks go inside lower set. Fit N/S frame on top of E/W frame before securing last track.

E/W

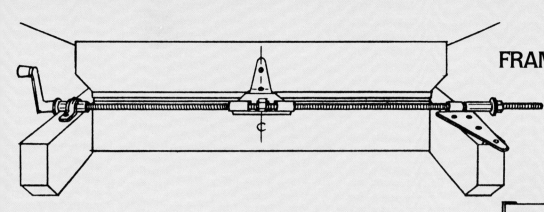

NORTH/SOUTH FRAME ATTACHMENT

(RIGHT SIDE VIEW)

(BACK VIEW)

Determine the center mark and fasten the north-south adjustment rod in the same manner as the east-west rod. NOTE: No acrylic plate is necessary in this fitting.

Lower the top of the compound onto the tracks and crank the control bracket (held by hand in photo) to center.

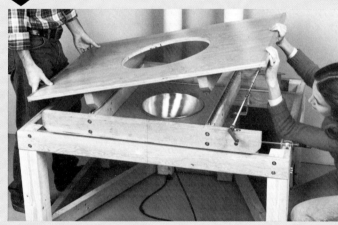

As on the east-west frame, the tracks on the north-south frame overlap with the top tracks on the inside to prevent sliding. (See the drawing on the opposite page.)

Crank the control bracket to the center of the north-south frame, and fasten the hinge mount to the center line.

ANIMATION DISK

If the disc is selected, cut a circular hole with a router in the exact center of the compound top. Make the first cut ⅛-inch deep and large enough to accommodate the outside diameter of the disc with no wobble. Allow a ⅜-inch shelf and cut the second groove straight through the top. Now, install the disc. The peg bars on the disc should not rest on the compound top.

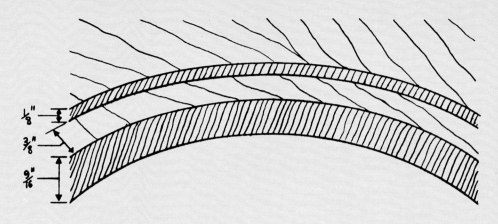

NOTE:
If you don't have a router, any local lumber yard could do this for you.

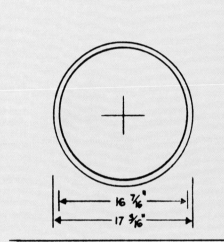

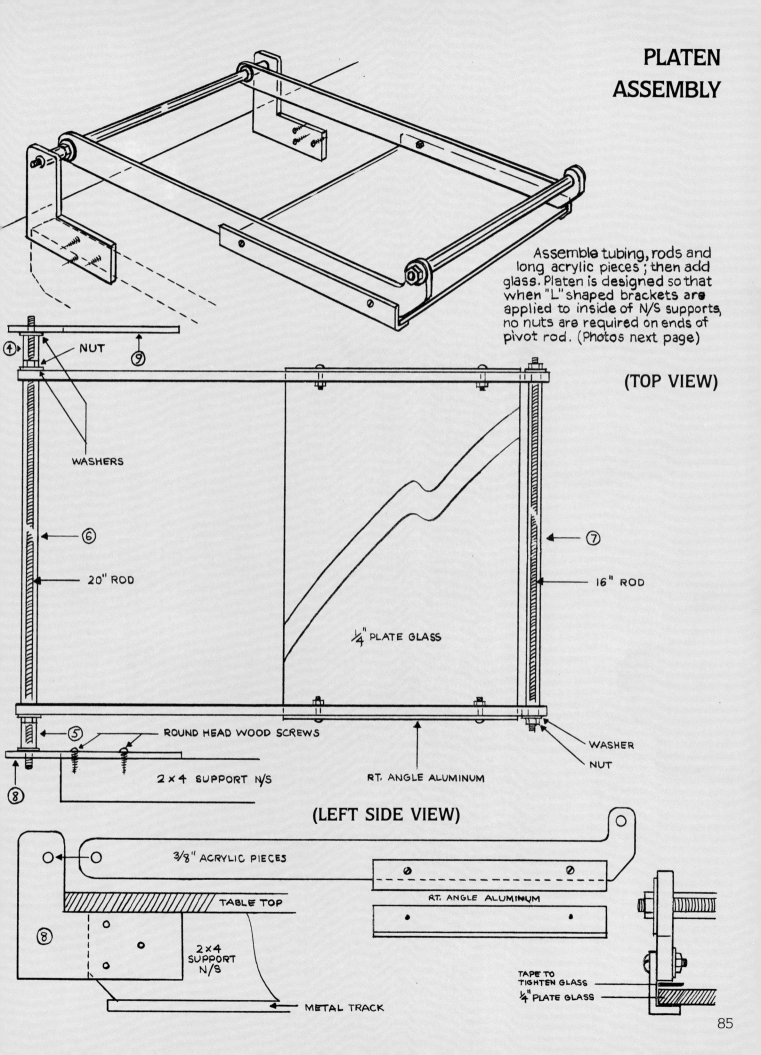

PLATEN ASSEMBLY

Assemble tubing, rods and long acrylic pieces ; then add glass. Platen is designed so that when "L" shaped brackets are applied to inside of N/S supports, no nuts are required on ends of pivot rod. (Photos next page)

(TOP VIEW)

④

NUT

⑨

WASHERS

⑥

20" ROD

⑦

16" ROD

¼" PLATE GLASS

⑤

ROUND HEAD WOOD SCREWS

WASHER

NUT

⑧

2 × 4 SUPPORT N/S

RT. ANGLE ALUMINUM

(LEFT SIDE VIEW)

3/8" ACRYLIC PIECES

TABLE TOP

RT. ANGLE ALUMINUM

⑧

2×4 SUPPORT N/S

METAL TRACK

TAPE TO TIGHTEN GLASS

¼" PLATE GLASS

PLATEN
ATTACHMENT

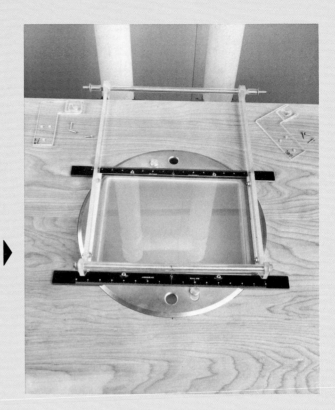

Place the platen in position over the disc after its construction (see drawings on preceding page). Using a "T square," line up pegs on bar to be parallel with the front edge of table and mark center.

Fasten the platen to the inside of the top of the compound (top frame), on the north-south support beam, with round-head wood screws or pan headed sheet metal screws.

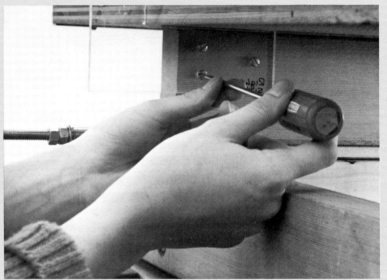

Now, place the ¼-inch thick foam pad between the disc and platen. This pad will help prevent buckling in cels and create a slight pressure to eliminate potential shadows on backgrounds.

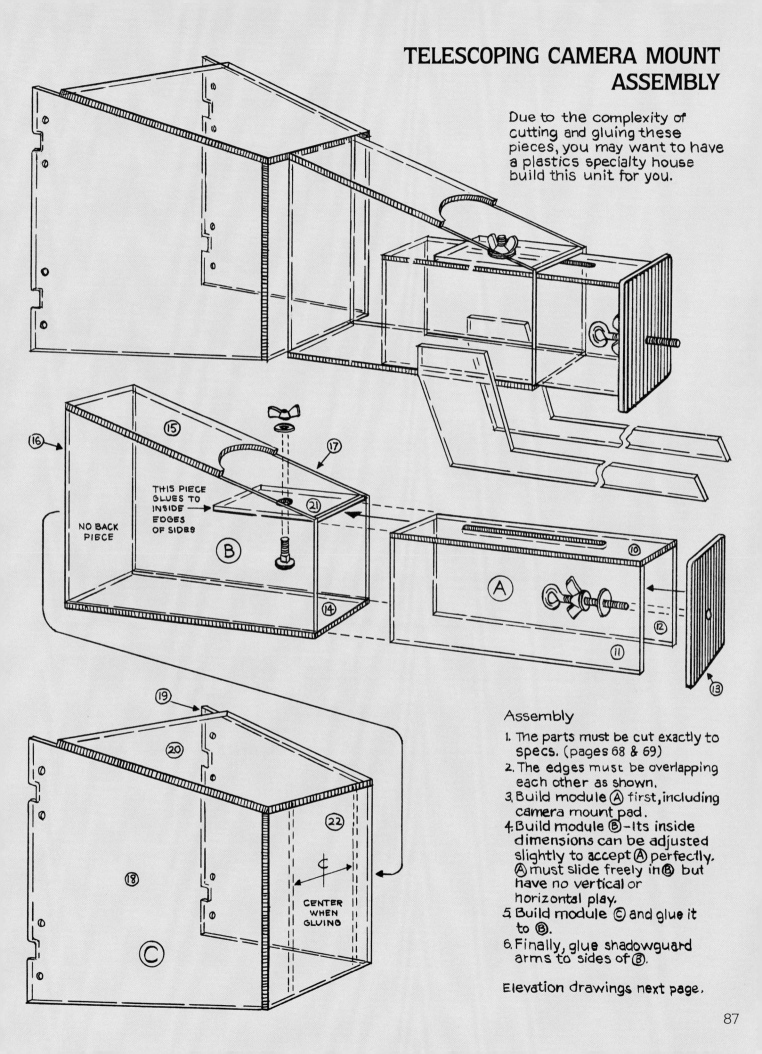

TELESCOPING CAMERA MOUNT ASSEMBLY

Due to the complexity of cutting and gluing these pieces, you may want to have a plastics specialty house build this unit for you.

⑮

⑯

⑰

THIS PIECE GLUES TO INSIDE EDGES OF SIDES

㉑

Ⓑ

⑭

NO BACK PIECE

⑩

Ⓐ

⑫

⑪

⑬

⑲

⑳

㉒

⑱

Ⓒ

₵

CENTER WHEN GLUING

Assembly

1. The parts must be cut exactly to specs. (pages 68 & 69)
2. The edges must be overlapping each other as shown.
3. Build module Ⓐ first, including camera mount pad.
4. Build module Ⓑ—Its inside dimensions can be adjusted slightly to accept Ⓐ perfectly. Ⓐ must slide freely in Ⓑ but have no vertical or horizontal play.
5. Build module Ⓒ and glue it to Ⓑ.
6. Finally, glue shadowguard arms to sides of Ⓑ.

Elevation drawings next page.

TELESCOPING CAMERA MOUNT

(ELEVATION DRAWINGS)

These drawings include the
attachment of the camera
mount to the camera mount
sleeves as detailed on page 76.

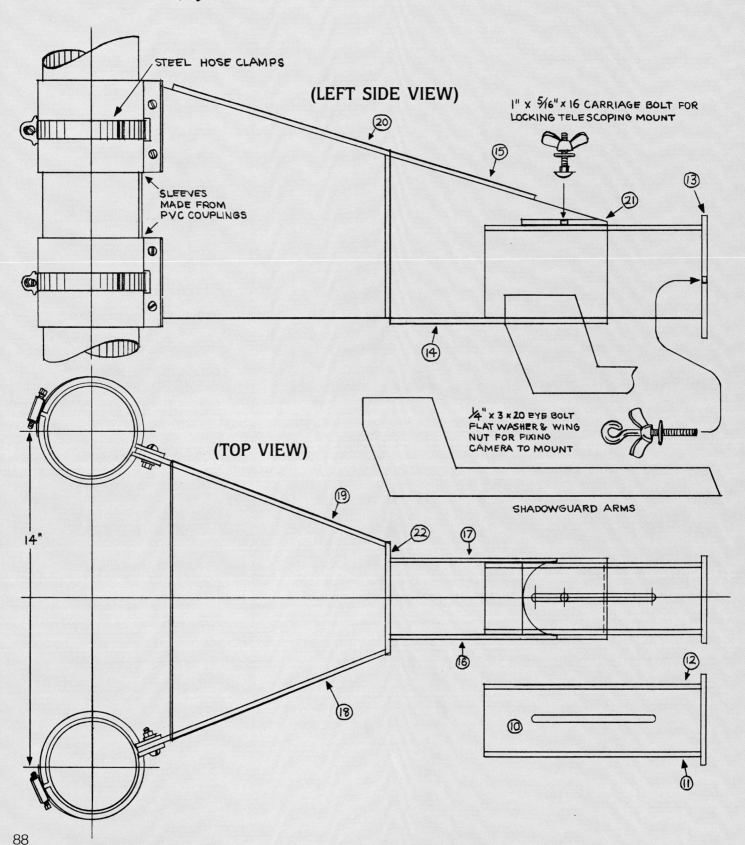

STEEL HOSE CLAMPS

(LEFT SIDE VIEW)

1" x 5/16" x 16 CARRIAGE BOLT FOR
LOCKING TELESCOPING MOUNT

SLEEVES
MADE FROM
PVC COUPLINGS

(TOP VIEW)

1/4" x 3 x 20 EYE BOLT
FLAT WASHER & WING
NUT FOR FIXING
CAMERA TO MOUNT

SHADOWGUARD ARMS

14"

TELESCOPING CAMERA MOUNT ATTACHMENT

Assemble the acrylic telescoping camera mount (see drawings on previous pages). Then fasten the mount to the sleeve on the PVC pipe using the 4-inch couplings and hose clamps shown on page 88, and ⅛-inch x ¾-inch machine screws and nuts.

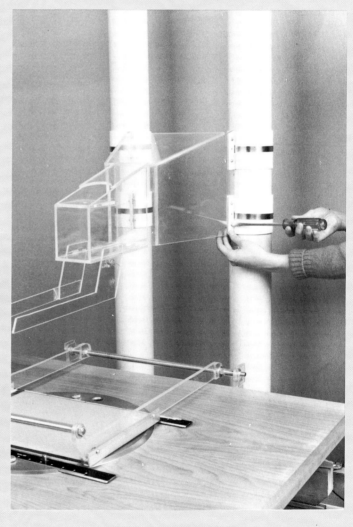

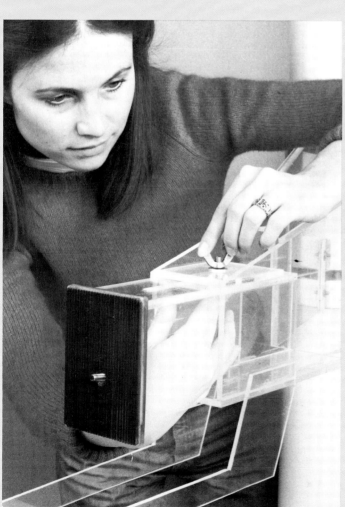

Fit the telescoping section into the camera carrier and fasten with a ⅜-inch x 1-inch carriage bolt, locking with a ⅜-inch wing nut and flat washer.

PANTOGRAPH ASSEMBLY

(RIGHT SIDE VIEW)

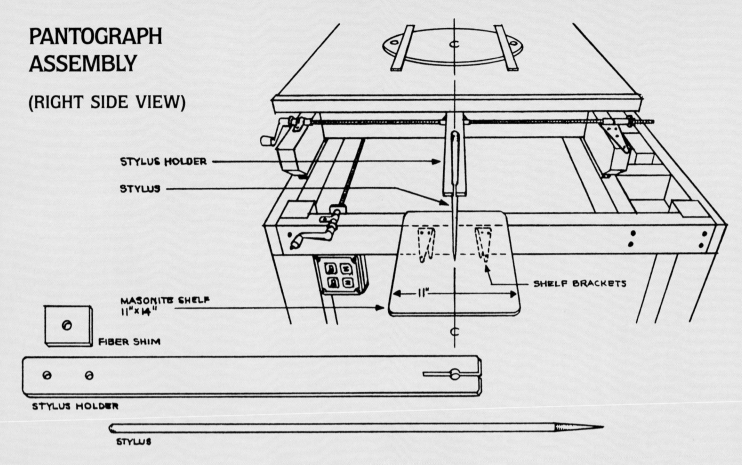

STYLUS HOLDER

STYLUS

SHELF BRACKETS

MASONITE SHELF 11" x 14"

11"

FIBER SHIM

STYLUS HOLDER

STYLUS

For the pantograph, fasten the two 4-in x 6-in right-angle shelf brackets to the side beam on both sides of the center mark that indicates the disc center on the compound top.

Now, fasten the Masonite-board shelf to the beam with the center mark on the beam matching the center line on the shelf (check it with a "T square").

Next, mount the pantograph stylus holder to the underside of the compound in the exact center.

Place a small fiberboard shim between the top of the stylus holder and the compound to compensate for the thickness of the metal edge.

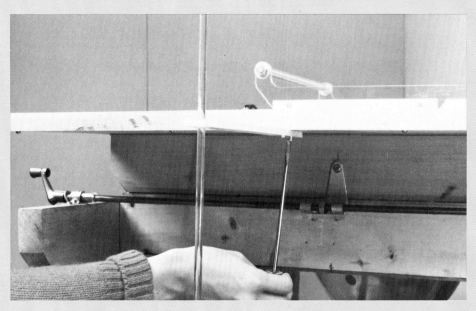

Now, place the stylus in the holder and adjust its position to the center line on the shelf. Then, lock it in position with a second screw.

Tape down a field guide and center it below the stylus, matching the center line with the line on the shelf. You can purchase a field guide from an animation supply house or a camera equipment dealer, or you can make your own.

Check the north-south and east-west travel by turning the cranks to be sure the field guide is straight and level as the stylus travels on the lines.

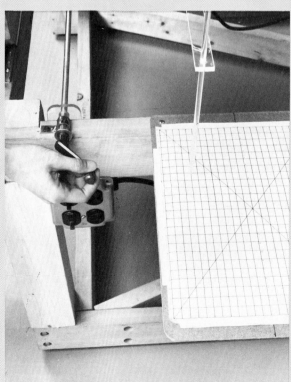

ANCHORING TO WALL

Firmly anchor the top of the vertical pipes to the wall behind the stand with steel bands and right angle braces to prevent camera vibration.

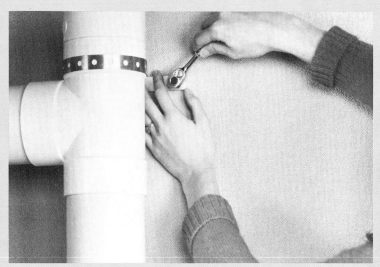

CAMERA MOUNTING

Now, mount the camera to the telescoping camera carrier with a standard ¼-inch x 3-inch x 16-inch eyebolt and lock it with a wing nut.

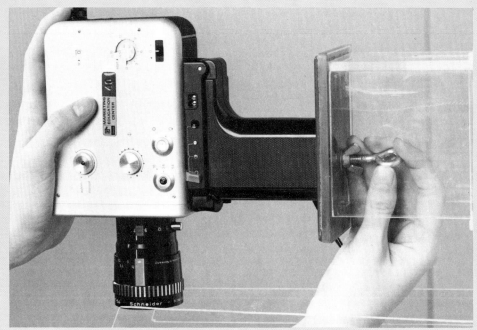

SELECTING A CAMERA FOR YOUR ANIMATION STAND

There are many used cameras for sale in photo equipment and supply stores, both super 8 and 16 mm. If you're interested in super 8, try to find a used one such as the discontinued KODAK EKTAGRAPHIC 8 Camera with single-frame capability. Prices range from $50 on up depending on the camera's condition. If you choose to use a 16 mm camera the larger gauge film will be easier to work with and more can be done with optical effects. Similar to the super 8 camera, the 16 mm camera should also be set up for single-frame filming and if at all possible, frame counting. There are old Bolex cameras and Bell & Howell Eyemo cameras available in the $66-$300 range depending on source and condition.

A reflex camera should be chosen to avoid parallax problems. The animator must know the field being filmed so it is advisable to have the reflex feature or at least a rackover system. Check with your dealer for a used camera that has been used for animation or that can be set up for animation with comparative case and economy.

The camera used in the photo above was a Bolex camera with a single-frame motor and frame counter. It was used but serviceable, and offered a reflex system—desirable qualities for animation shooting on an economy setup.

FINAL LEVELING

Rotate the ⅜-inch x 3-inch machine bolts and nuts in the corners of the base to adjust the table level. Use a leveler to assure an even compound top.

 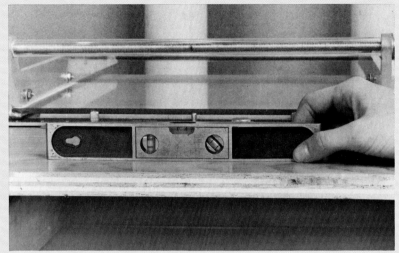

LIGHTING

Assemble the tripod lamps; these lamps are for top lighting on the compound and should be adjusted so that the light rays are at a 45-degree angle to the art being filmed.

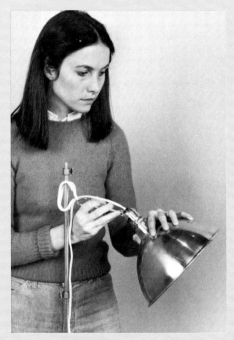

SHADOWGUARD

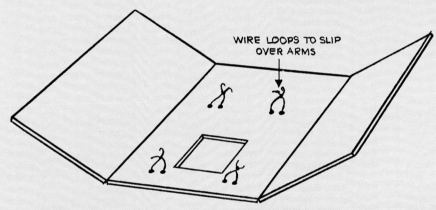

WIRE LOOPS TO SLIP OVER ARMS

The last step is to make a shadow guard out of foamcore (or another light material) and paint it matte black on the side that faces the art and light. Also, position it so that the lens window is below the lens.

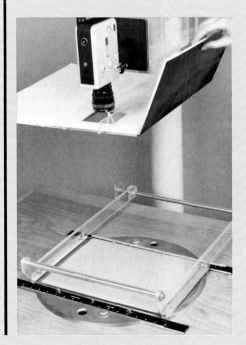

PART FIVE

How to Budget for Animation

You'll find that animation costs vary from film to film, according to the length, techniques used, and the skill level of manpower applied. Because these considerations change with each new production, it is necessary to have some means of calculating what you can expect to spend. Of course, working out a budget is done before production of your animated sequence even begins. But by placing these budget considerations at this point in the book, you are now more familiar with your needs and the costs you will incur.

There are several ways to compute costs for animation, but the easiest way is to determine all of the elements that will be applied to your production, and then break down the cost factor into an itemized list. For example:

1. **Script** and other writing, such as proposals, rationals, scenarios . . . . _____

2. **Raw film stock**, determined by length of script, and safely multiplied by a 3 to 1 ratio . . . . _____

3. **Manpower.** How many people? How much time? Multiply their time versus weekly rate. (i.e., 4 wks x $371) for each . . . . _____

   NOTE: In some nonunion areas, the individual is paid by the amount of footage produced. (i.e., $55 per foot). This specifically applies to animators.

4. **Sound track.** Voice casting, talent, music, sound effects, recording studio, rerecording (mixing), analysis (usually by editor), transfers (dubs) . . . . _____

5. **Materials.** Paper, drawing utensils, acetate (cels), paints, gloves . . . . _____

6. **Equipment.** Stand, special effects gear, lamps, filters, accessories, extra boards, stools, etc . . . . _____

7. **Postproduction.** Editing and lab., including answer and release prints . . . . _____

8. **Distribution.** A necessary consideration to make sure that the film receives proper exposure and usage. May include direct-mail brochures, trade advertising, sales promotion, public relations and the number of release prints required for the promotion program . . . . _____

As you have already learned, time (either yours or those you hire) is your most costly consideration. Actually very little film is used, and although the cost of materials is rising each year, it isn't very expensive to create an animated sequence using your own labor. For instance, if your only expenses are for materials, you can create a simple, one-minute commercial spot (at the rate of two frames per cel) for approximately $150, based on the current material costs listed below. (Film processing not included.)

Here's a list of the basic items (and associated costs*) you need to know about:

Animation bond paper, punched, 12-field size, for pencil drawings, 1000 sheets	$ 22.00
Acetate cels, 12-field size, punched, 1000 sheets	118.00
Opaque black ink, for use on acetate cels, 1 oz.	1.50
Rapidograph pen with one point size	16.00
Cotton inking gloves	.50
Basic set of 8 colors, 2-oz bottles	14.60
Background Bristol paper, 12-field size, punched, one piece	.40
Background color cards, 12-field, 10 assorted colors	2.00
Animation exposure sheet pad, 50 sheets	2.50
Field guide, 12-field size, punched	4.00
Paint brushes	3.75 to 13.25
	(depending on size)

NOTE: For a more in-depth look at the business side of filmmaking, refer to Kodak's publication, **THE BUSINESS OF FILMMAKING** (H-55).

*Prices based on 1978 figures.

PART SIX

Why and Where Animation is Used

Television Commercials

Because animation has a wide range of applications, styles and techniques, it lends itself very well to commercial messages. In fact, so powerful is animation for selling that advertising pros all over the world frequently use it whenever a "punch" is essential for pushing a product, service, or corporate concept. The largest amount of animation for commercials is being done within the United States in New York City and Los Angeles. However, very fine animation is also done for television commercials in numerous other countries including Great Britain, France, and Italy.

TV animation for commercials is done using most of the techniques already mentioned in this book, with cel being the most prominent and puppet running a close second. And although commercial animation began with one-minute spots during the early days of television, animators now work primarily on half-minute spots that are actually about 26 seconds of production.

While entertainment animation studios such as DePatie-Freleng and Richard Williams Animation Limited can do fine work for commercial messages, along with shorts and feature films that make up the majority of their work, most commercial animation studios specialize in this area alone and rarely venture into entertainment animation or lengthy productions of any kind. A studio that has enjoyed much success in commercial animation is Kurtz and Friends, in Los Angeles. Kurtz and Friends' TV ads have won numerous awards and received high acclaim from their professional peers for their visual inventiveness. One example of their award-winning talent is a commercial done for Sears to advertise shoes for sports. The athletic figures in the spot contribute to the motion and dynamics, but fall to the background in a wide-angle perspective to emphasize the product.

This frame from a Kurtz & Friends' TV spot for Sears reveals this animation studio's talent for design impact and dynamics.

A knowledgeable frog and company demonstrate the features of a Buster Brown shoe in a humorous and effective spot created by Filmfair, Inc. and Darcy-McManus & Massius, Inc. for the Buster Brown Div. of the Brown Shoe Co.

Currently, the most prominent American commercial animation houses are located on the east coast with Phil Kimmelman and Zander's Animation Parlor heading the list. Also worthy of mention are Perpetual Motion Pictures, Image Factory, Inc., and IF Studios Inc. Computer animation is also offered by studios such as Dolphin Productions, Zeplin, and Magi. Although all of these animators are located in New York, there are other top talents located in other parts of the country as well. Not to be overlooked are Bajus-Jones in Minneapolis and New York; Filmfair, Inc., in Chicago, New York, Los Angeles, and London; and Rick Reinert Productions in Cleveland and Los Angeles. The frames shown from Bajus-Jones are a good example of how a very simple line technique can result in an entertaining and persuasive commercial. In this case, bank loan services are promoted. This portion of the film shows a character who is dreaming of flying away for a vacation. As he thinks about the plane that will take him away, he calls his bank to arrange for a loan. By the end of the conversation, he obtains his loan and the "dream plane" turns from a thought into a reality.

Turning to the west coast where, if you only count all the studios doing commercials outside the city of Los Angeles, you will find a greater production volume than in New York City, there is a great

Here's an example of cel animation done for Lincoln First Bank, created by Hutchins/Y&R and Bajus-Jones Film Corporation.

variety in approaches to animation, and much diversity in style and graphics. Along with the previously mentioned Dick Williams and Bob Kurtz and Friends, there are many studios that take numerous assignments including animated TV commercials. Some of them are Murakami Wolf Swenson Films, Inc.; Bill Melendez, who has done all the PEANUTS SPECIALS, but also does commercial spots; Gallerie International Films, which frequently combines live action with animation; and CPC Associates, which uses the talents of the great Tex Avery of Bugs Bunny fame.

Studios that use special effects for commercial messages, such as Robert Abel & Associates and Gehring Aviation (both located in Los Angeles), also belong in this commercial animation group, even though they work in areas other than cels or puppets. Special effects studios film art and optical images, layering one on top of another, exactly like a modern sound studio with a 24-track tape recorder. The end result is glimmering cinema magic on one composite image that is dynamic and exciting to view over and over again. These very fine effects have been noticed by the young directors in Hollywood and used in some of the fantasy films such as STAR WARS and television's genre copy BATTLESTAR GALACTICA.

Some very creative commercial animation spots are also being done in Canada by studios such as Nelvana, Cinera Productions, Film Design, Rainbow Animation and M. S. Art Services in Toronto and Animation Productions in Moffat, Ontario.

In terms of production costs, animation spots are in healthy competition with live action. If you create 12 or more camera-ready cels (including backgrounds) for each second of film, the art preparation is more time-consuming than live-action shooting, but the overall cost of a live-action commercial ends up being equal to or more expensive than an animated one because residuals have to be paid to actors in the live-action spots.

And if a live-action spot is done on a grand scale to have the "look" of a major film theatrical release that has captured public fancy, a production with a large cast, complex action, and exotic locations will make the spot even more expensive.

Price quotes from major animation and live action studios indicate that the final production costs are close to equal, even without actors' residuals added in for the live action spots. Prices for animated spots quoted by producers in major cities run from $4,000 to $20,000 for 30 seconds of animation and prices quoted for live action run from $3,000 to $25,000 (not including actors' residuals).

In addition to being financially competitive with live action, an animated commercial offers other advantages, too, such as a tremendous amount of flexibility of motion to make points in a severely limited time span. It also has a long life span because the characters and situations aren't dated as quickly as those in live action. Many animated commercials produced ten years ago are still fresh and informative today. And animation has a great deal of refreshing entertainment value giving it a high repeatability factor. For the animator, animation offers an unlimited scope of creative application. Some say that the only disadvantage is lack of audience identification with major characters—but that "disadvantage" is one that Walt Disney would have laughed at.

Public Relations Films

For the same basic reasons that animation is potent in television commercials, corporations, institutions, and government agencies use it frequently to communicate with their various audiences. Animation is particularly effective for public relations films because it has the ability to convey a very human element that appeals to the emotions of the viewer as it entertains. A fine example is the Rick Reinert film for O'Neil's shown in storyboard form. This cel-animated film promotes shopping at O'Neil's as a natural part of the holiday season. It would be very difficult to find a warmer, more delightful film treatment. Even though public relations films are often done in live action for reasons of expediency, the effectiveness of animated films is well established and interest seems to be growing. The animated films that have been done include short spots for 30 seconds and some lengthier ones in the 15- to 25-minute category.

A storyboard produced by Rick Reinert Productions for O'Neil's department store.

O'NEIL'S
"CHRISTMAS"

Animation by:
Rick Reinert
Penton, Inc.

ANNCR: Christmas is seeing your breath

and snow flakes.

Christmas is laughter and joy.

And shopping for presents.

Christmas is for Grampas and Grandmas,

Moms and Dads

And kids

Even Cats and Dogs.

And Hamsters

But mostly kids...

Christmas is giving gifts.

In fact,

Christmas is a gift.

And Christmas is a tradition at O'Neil's

VOCAL REFRAIN: At O'Neil's where it's happening now...

As animation continues to gain public acceptance and a wider following, there's little doubt that corporations, institutions, and agencies of federal and state governments and private organizations desiring to communicate their particular message to their audiences will increasingly turn to this special medium. An excellent example is the clay animation in the film "Oregonians for Nuclear Safeguards," created by Bob Gardiner Animation and Illustration in Portland. The purpose of this film was to attract attention to a political issue coming up in an election. The votable issue was whether or not to have tighter safety measures and better pre-planning before the building of proposed nuclear plants is decided. The reflective river is made of Mylar and the cooling tower has a device built underneath that turns and tilts the tower incrementally in any direction. The set was built within several weeks and the lighting and shooting was done in the two weeks that followed. Gardiner thinks clay sculpting is cheaper than other animation techniques and saves time, too. The dynamics of his animation or "sculptimation," as he likes to call it, is evident in the examples shown. "Sculptimation," says Gardiner, "is fresh and attracts attention." He adds, "It is also inherently humorous which provides a vital scope when dealing with sensitive or serious issues."

"OREGONIANS FOR NUCLEAR SAFEGUARDS," created through the efforts of the Ted Hallock Agency, the Film Loft, and producer/animator/sculptor J.R. "Bob" Gardiner, shows the highly effective use of clay animation in this public information spot.

Training and Educational Films

Many instructional films contain animated segments to demonstrate the operation of systems, processes, organisms, and organizations—subjects that could not be shown in any other way but with animation. Animation provides a simplified look at structure from any perspective desired. A good example of how effective animation can be is an educational film produced for Eastman Kodak Company by Jim Mackay from Film Design in Toronto. The film entitled "How Photography Works" shows information on choosing depth of field, focusing, advancing film, and other procedures that are difficult or impossible to show in live-action footage. The frames in the example show the procedure for split-image focusing. By using animation, the student has a simulated view of how to align an image while looking through the viewfinder of a camera.

For engineering purposes, no other film technique permits the breakdown and analysis of systems or processes so effectively

as animation. Further, theoretical systems that exist only in the imagination of the designer can adequately be illustrated with this creative medium. Imagine someone developing a nuclear reactor containing major technological breakthroughs. What better presentation platform than an animated film could there be to show things that cannot be filmed in live-action. So irresistible are training films to animators that even the Disney studio has produced them. And animation lends itself to science studies so well that many filmmakers have spent much of their lives animating this type of information.

As stated earlier, animation is not just entertaining cartoons. It can provide an in-depth view of how the human anatomy operates, or how an ecological system maintains its awesome balance. Animation can also provide a comprehensive study of a weather cycle, cellular mitosis, the surface of a neighboring planet, and endless other topics that can fascinate and more effectively educate when animated.

Jim Mackay's art from Film Design in Toronto is a fine example of how useful animation can be for educational films.

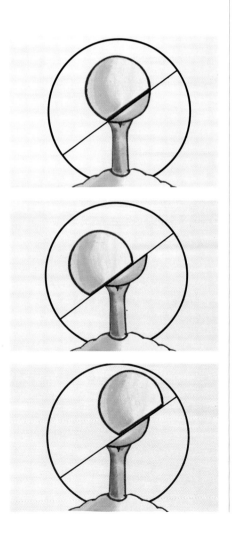

Raoul Servais, writer, director, and animator as "fine artist," has found the animated film to have unlimited flexibility for expression. Servais is the winner of over 40 national and international awards for animated films . . . all personal statements.

Art Films

Within each of us exists the natural need for self-expression and that is what art films are all about. Also known as experimental or avant-garde films, they express man's dreams, nightmares, hopes, fears, anxieties, wit . . . all aspects of the human condition. These films are universal in nature, but do not usually have general theatre audience appeal, so they come from all corners of the world to a platform that willingly accepts them . . . the film festival.

At film festivals, audiences are usually communicated to on a high creative level by talented innovators. Some films are so freeform and abstract that they miss the communication mark. The art film not only allows expression, but also seeds the creative minds in the audience; it is a creative exchange between the creator and the audience.

Many experimental films are very stark and simple, with no backgrounds, and consist mainly of line animation. Others are filled with innovative visual poetry. Films of this latter type are made by artists like Belgium's Raoul Servais, who presently heads the animated film department at the Royal Academy of Fine Arts in Ghent and teaches at the National School of Visual Arts in Brussels.

Although Raoul Servais studied applied arts at the Ghent Academy, he was 32 years of age before he realized that animation offered life to his art. From that point, he exploded forth with a brilliant creative output of intense statements which are, at the same time, universal in nature and appeal. With eight films, he has won more than forty national and international awards, gaining high acclaim in the United States and Belgium. In CHROMOPHOBIA, a Servais film released in 1966, a black-and-white army attempts to impose its dictatorial rule on a free, happy, colorful society.

Where the gray legions pass, all color disappears. A small girl nurtures one red flower left untouched that eventually takes the shape of a scarlet jester, Tyl Uylenspiegel. This jester, a remnant of color and spirit, helps the people to overcome the invader and restore their free, color-filled world. The film, like almost all of Servais films, has no narrative. Instead, it uses clever and whimsical animation and music to tell its tale of suppression, fear, and the ultimate victory of the free spirit. The film won awards in Italy, Iran, Canada, France, Spain, Belgium, East Germany, and Russia.

In Servais' SIRENE, released in 1968, the theme changes, but again, social relevance is the platform. SIRENE is an alarming and frightful film filled with monstrous cranes and winged antediluvian reptiles that dominate an inhospitable harbor. A solitary fisherman

Scene from Raoul Servais' SIRENE—a film filled with a haunting sequence of images that create an impact upon the human consciousness.

In Servais' multiple award winner, CHROMOPHOBIA, we see an example of design elements that serve to project the symbolic language employed by the artist. Color, as always, plays a major role, but in this film color plays the lead role.

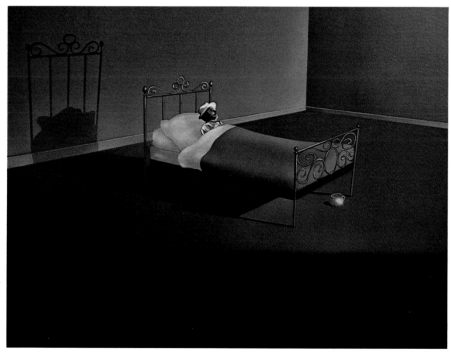

The latest film from Raoul Servais, HARPYA, reflects a surreal landscape which is symbolic of the dark corners of the human consciousness, a subject reached best with film animation techniques—particularly the techniques of this Belgian artist. This film won the 1979 Grand Prix award at the Cannes Film Festival.

is the only human allowed to remain in the area—he is to witness a theft, a police investigation, and finally a Solomonian judgment.

Next to one of the docks in this Dantesque harbor, an enchanted three-masted windjammer is kept captive. Her sole crew, a cabin boy, falls in love with the figurehead at the bow of the ship—a mermaid who suddenly comes to life. Is it a dream? Or is it reality? It doesn't matter. The authorities destroy the mermaid . . . but they do not destroy her spirit, which returns to bring the hope of rescue and freedom. This film won awards in Iran, the United States, Australia, France, and Belgium.

Because animation offers an added dimension to personal expression, it is perhaps one of the most satisfying of all art forms. If the expression is universal enough and defies dating, as most of the Servais films do, the animator as a fine artist can create a timeless statement. Servais' films are direct, hard-hitting fare that penetrate what he thinks are superficial mores that allow no room for freedom of expression. In no other medium can the artist stimulate the emotion and conscience of the viewer with the immediacy and impact of an animated film.

Creative contributions are also made by students such as Donald Fox who, almost a decade ago, as a UCLA student, created OMEGA with almost no education in special effects and no practical field experience. The film has been heralded as one of the best experimental films of all times . . . made by a young man who knew no limitations. He built his own animation stand, his own rotoscope, and used a borrowed printer. The classic film is still in distribution today.

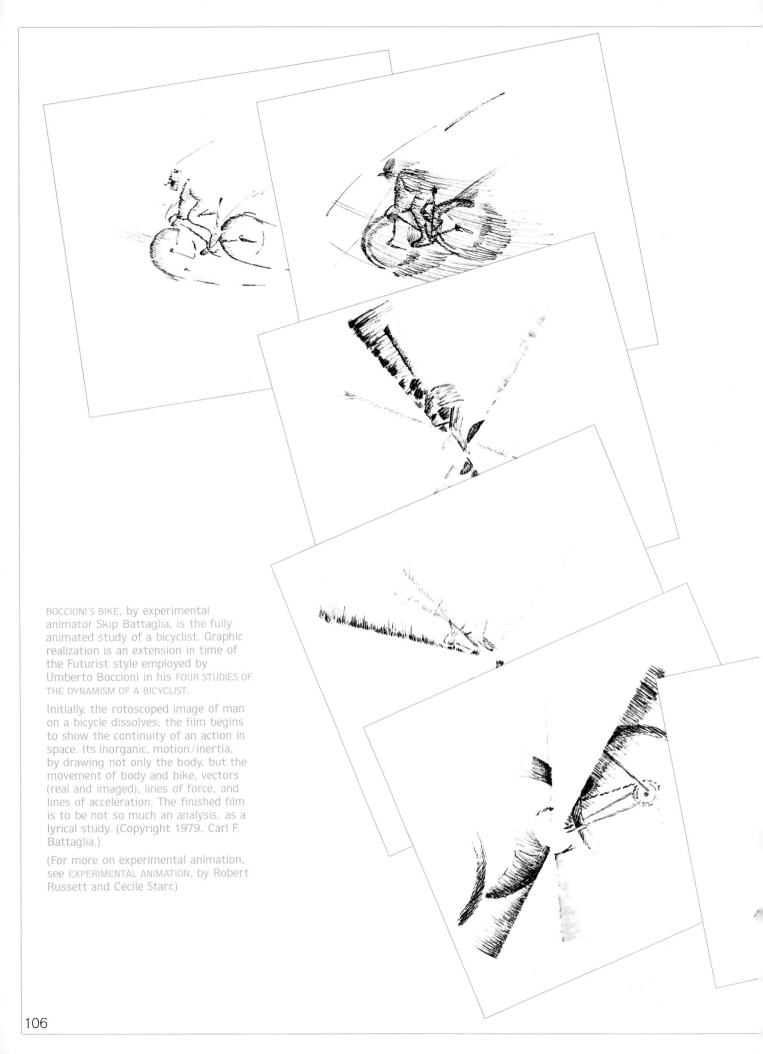

BOCCIONI'S BIKE, by experimental
animator Skip Battaglia, is the fully
animated study of a bicyclist. Graphic
realization is an extension in time of
the Futurist style employed by
Umberto Boccioni in his FOUR STUDIES OF
THE DYNAMISM OF A BICYCLIST.

Initially, the rotoscoped image of man
on a bicycle dissolves; the film begins
to show the continuity of an action in
space. Its inorganic, motion/inertia,
by drawing not only the body, but the
movement of body and bike, vectors
(real and imaged), lines of force, and
lines of acceleration. The finished film
is to be not so much an analysis, as a
lyrical study. (Copyright 1979, Carl F.
Battaglia.)

(For more on experimental animation,
see EXPERIMENTAL ANIMATION, by Robert
Russett and Cecile Starr.)

Other recognized artists include those in the Yugoslav Zagreb Film Company. The extraordinary creativity of this company is now world famous. The company, formed in 1956, produces stinging social satire and comedy in mini-portions of 30 seconds to one minute each that have the impact of a keg of dynamite. The Zagreb Film Studio product is often the highlight of international film and animation festivals, almost always winning top awards.

Within the rapidly growing Yugoslav film industry, the animated films of Zagreb are the most brilliant. What is the secret of the Zagreb school? The animators began with no knowledge of animation. With the barest of material resources, they learned from their own mistakes and successes; one of the most ingenious being their own famous technique of reduced animation (a form of limited animation retaining expressive movement while reducing the number of drawings necessary to achieve the desired visual effect). Artists in other media—sculptors, writers, composers, painters, set designers—were sought out to lend their talents and share their ideas. Yet, if you ask an artist at Zagreb the reason for such an uncommon pool of creativity and professionalism, he will reply with a twinkle in his eye, "Well, maybe it's the coffee shop in our backyard." In this very modest, crowded, family-like environment, artists and technicians play, discuss, argue, and share ideas and information. The coffee also has a reputation for being good. One can imagine that this is the way it was at the Warner Brothers animation units of the 40s and 50s . . . the peak of that studio's productive period.

The long-time head of Zagreb Film, Dusan Vuokotic has said, "We do know that the cartoon film is an art as limitless as imagination itself. And within this immense sphere there is surely enough room for all kinds of emotion, for any ventures of man's mind, and not only for fun and entertainment."

What distinguishes the films is a satirical wit, experimentation with modern graphic forms and composition, color harmony, and contrapuntal use of music and sound effects. Most of the films are fables, with all the charm and humor of Aesop or La Fontaine. They are visual delights that enchant the imagination of any age.

Experimental animation can come from all walks of life . . . not just from professionals and semiprofessionals aspiring to creative recognition, but from serious experimenters who have made their lifework elsewhere and seek to use animation as a means of self-expression. The reasons are myriad. Most will agree, however, that it is difficult to pit one of these types of film against another because of their subjective nature, which is why most festivals are expository in nature and competition is kept at a minimum.

Here are some final words about animation from the artists of the Zagreb studio:

"Animation is . . . a protest against the stationary condition."

"To animate: to give life and soul to a design, not through the copying but through the transformation of reality."

"Life is warmness.
Warmness is movement.
Movement is life.
Animation is giving life;
it means giving warmth."

"Practically, animation is a long rubbing of tree against tree in order to get sparkle or perhaps just a little smoke."

The Theatrical Short Subject

There was a time when major film production studios distributed their own films. Along with the feature-length production, there were also cartoon shorts that were usually about six minutes long. Most of us can recall that period, and there are still areas where animated cartoon shorts can still be seen with a feature, but the practice appears to be dying out largely for financial reasons. It is this cartoon short that gave life to animation as we know it today and introduced us to the major talents of that time: Walter Lanz, Paul Terry, the Fleischer brothers, the Warner Brothers studio, MGM, the great Disney studio of the 30s and 40s, and others. Virtually every pioneer learned animation by working on theatrical shorts. The last American pioneer still working on theatrical shorts is Friz Freleng of DePatie-Freleng, who has produced THE ANT AND THE AARDVARK, THE PINK PANTHER, and several others.

In Canada, hundreds of shorts and documentaries have been created and are popular for use in schools. Two particularly witty, animated film shorts for children were created by Canadian writer/director Co Hoedeman. Both films are in color and are thirteen minutes long. One film, called TCHOU-TCHOU, uses little block characters made up of three blocks. (A head, a body, and legs) each of which can move independently from the other two. The story is about a game two children play with a dragon. The other Hoedeman film, SANDCASTLE, uses molded sand creatures as its animated characters. A 1978 Oscar winner, this humorous film deals with the birth, death and rebirth of the world.

One of the last great pioneers, Isadore "Friz" Freleng, is still making audiences laugh with these theatrical shorts—Depatie-Freleng's THE ANT AND THE AARDVARK and THE PINK PANTHER.

Children's Entertainment for Television

The same greats that lost the market for the theatrical short turned to television—the voracious electronic system that, today, devours many hours of animation per week. Because of the medium's requirements for half-hour segments for modest sums of money, some animators have turned to limited-motion animation for economic survival. The only major studio not in the KidVid business is Disney. The Disney studio relies mostly on their large library of fine theatrical animation, which they have used for their own weekly television program that is now approaching its 25-year anniversary. All of the films are fully animated (as opposed to limited motion) and are created especially for the program, including exerpts from their feature-length films.

Most of the studios working on television programs have talented artists on staffs and the ability to produce fine animation. Indeed, some are expanding their offerings into specials that run half an hour and over into the feature-length area for television. Hanna-Barbera, the largest producer of television animation or KidVid, is working on HEIDI'S SONG, a 90-minute special for television; Filmation's feature special is FLASH GORDON; and DePatie-Freleng is working on a PINK PANTHER special. All of these will have been broadcast by the time this book is in print and others are undoubtedly now in the planning and production stages.

The Feature-Length Film

In his book FULL-LENGTH ANIMATED FEATURE FILMS, Bruno Edera lists seven animated films in the feature-length category prior to Disney's first production, SNOW WHITE AND THE SEVEN DWARFS, in 1938. Of the seven, three are actually cel cartoon types, the first completed in 1917. This first feature-length, animated film, produced in Argentina by Frederico Valle, was called THE APOSTLE and was a political satire about President Irigoyen of Argentina. Quirino Cristiani, one of the key animators on THE APOSTLE, made yet another satirical film on the same subject in 1931. Because Disney's first feature length film was so completely different from anything done previously, it was a great gamble. The gamble, however, was made somewhat secure by the sheer output of art excellence, superb music, and fine character development in addition to the use of a universally appealing plot filled with timeless symbols. In short, Disney pulled out all the stops for his first full-length film and he put forth his best efforts for effective international distribution. It is this flair for trying a new concept that's exciting and different which has helped Disney lead the field for such a long time.

Once a studio such as Disney establishes a convention, investors or backers for new film ideas can become fearful of breaking new ground. Quite often, a fine film is released with inadequate investor confidence and, in many cases, the film is not properly promoted.

Such was the case with Max and Dave Fleischer's two early Paramount films following Disney's SNOW WHITE AND THE SEVEN DWARFS. The first was GULLIVER'S TRAVELS, a Jonathan Swift satire released in 1939 and 1940. The second used an original story by Dave Fleischer, who also served as director of the film called MR. BUG GOES TO TOWN (1941), later released as HOPPITY GOES TO TOWN. Although the films evidenced a different style and quality than the Disney art, they were fine examples of animated film entertainment for that period. Unfortunately, the films were released without much fanfare and were not commercial successes. As time passes, interest is building and the films have now been released on television. They will undoubtedly become more popular as they become recognized for their special entertainment value.

Since the late thirties the Disney studio has dominated the feature-length film market with its fine animated films in the continuing tradition of entertainment for children. However, within the past ten years other well-known studios have produced and are currently producing some highly creative work as well. In 1972, Hanna-Barbera produced a feature-length, fully animated film for children entitled CHARLOTTE'S WEB. Bill Melendez recently released an animated version of C. S. Lewis' first book in the NARNIA CHRONICLES called THE LION, THE WITCH, AND THE WARDROBE. And Richard Williams Animation Limited produced a beautifully detailed film in 1972, based on Charles Dickens' A CHRISTMAS CAROL. Since then, he has also produced the feature-length film RAGGEDY ANN AND ANDY (1977), and his studio is currently working on THE THIEF

All of the above films have continued the Disney tradition of entertainment for children. Ralph Bakshi, on the other hand, has radically broken the "mold." In 1972 Bakshi, an independent animator in Los Angeles, made an end run with his racy FRITZ THE CAT and scored a touchdown because he tapped an entirely new audience at the right time with the right "nerve tonic." Reviews of his adult films since FRITZ THE CAT have been mixed, however, as controversy has welled up over his yet unreleased COONSKIN and to a lesser extent, HEAVY TRAFFIC, released in 1973. Bakshi's contribution to the feature-length animated film is a major one in that he broke tradition and paved the way for new animators to come in with a broad range of approaches to the art. His current production, THE LORD OF THE RINGS, based on the Tolkien work, exemplifies yet another direction for animated feature-length films geared toward adult audiences.

At the present time, there are about 50 other films in production around the world with more in the planning stages. The animated feature length film appears to have a bright future ahead.

CHARLOTTE'S WEB, one of Hanna-Barbera's full-length features, was released in 1972. The studio has plans for more features with HEIDI'S SONG in current release.

The Ghost of Christmas Present with Scrooge in a spectacular flying sequence from A CHRISTMAS CAROL.

A rare moment of rest among his laurels in London for Oscar-winning animator, Richard Williams, who won the award for his 1973 animated version of Charles Dicken's A CHRISTMAS CAROL.

PART SEVEN

The Production Personnel and Craftsmen: What They Do

The following discussion of the job titles and functions required in a typical animation studio will give you a basic idea of how such an organization operates. But keep in mind that there are no strict lines of division between titles; every studio's organization is a little different depending on the needs and philosophies of the people in charge.

The Producer

In financial terms, the producer is often the investor who comes up with the budget money. But in a case where there is an executive producer **and** a producer, the executive producer is usually the money raiser and also the one in charge, even if the administrative functions are shared. There are exceptions, however, where the person bearing the title "executive producer" has merely raised the investment money for the production and has delegated almost all of his or her responsibilities to the producer.

As mentioned at the beginning of this section, there are no strict lines of division between titles, particularly at the smaller studios. The large major studios usually have more clearly defined responsibilities than the smaller studios for reasons of efficiency, but an individual with the title "producer" at a small studio can easily be anything from director to checker or in-betweener. The small studios tend to have "pitch-in" teams who work hand-in-hand through every phase of production, and what function each individual is assigned can depend on the philosophy of the producer in charge. For example, Dick Williams of Richard Williams

Animation Limited will quite often work on any phase of production, in addition to serving as producer and creative director. Unlike Williams, Chuck Jones of Chuck Jones Enterprises runs his studio as producer/director and does not "get on the drawing board" as a rule. Jones feels that taking pencil in hand will rob him of creative direction time, while Dick Williams has an intense interest in contributing to each phase of the production.

Although there are variations from one production to another, the producer's responsibilities usually include acquiring the script, hiring the director and other key members of the crew and staff, and maintaining supervisory control over the production. He or she also controls the budget, maintains deadlines on delivery, and frequently consults with the director on creative matters. Ultimately, the producer is in charge of the administrative functions.

The Director

In general, a director is the person who translates the script into film reality and makes all the "creative" decisions. This individual is usually one who has mastered animation or has at least worked competently in most phases, from craftsman to conceptualizer and interpreter. The director often helps the producer with the selection of key animators and other personnel for the production, since he will be intimately involved with all the creative work performed.

It is the director who coordinates all phases of production—organizes the storyboard, instructs artists and supervises their work, serves as an idea person, and organizes the marriage of the sound track to the artwork.

Finally, the director is responsible for the overall quality of the production, even though this is the ultimate responsibility of the producer in the broadest sense.

The Character Designer

In animation, the character designer is very much like a casting director. He or she reads the script, "interprets" a character type, and then comes up with the right character to fit the requirements of the story. A character designer must have an understanding of anatomy and the wide range of facial expressions a character can show, and then be able to convey this understanding through life-like movements and expressions of the character he or she creates. He or she must also be able to come up with a character design that is easy to work with and still fits the character role in terms of appearance.

When a new character is created, the character designer uses a model sheet, mentioned in Part Two, to present the character to the director. Usually, three types of model sheets are made up for each character: one shows the character from all viewpoints, another shows the character with a variety of expressions, and a third shows the character's size relative to other characters in the story.

In addition to being drawn well, a new character must have a human appeal with which audiences can identify—the same kind of appeal that popularized one of the best-loved characters ever conceived: Mickey Mouse. This delightful character, with his endearing personality, has charmed audiences for more than fifty years and endures as an entity in himself. His happy face evokes instant identification and a smile from the millions who have enjoyed his antics.

The Layout Artist

Artists sometimes double up on duties, depending on their skills and experience, but to clarify the functions essential in the production phases of an animated film, here's a general breakdown of responsibilities.

The layout artist designs the "mood" or "atmosphere" sketches from which the background artist makes the background art. He or she also determines the size and space in which the animator must work and is, to a large extent, responsible for the general design of the film. Scene transitions, panning, zooms, and other motions of the camera or compound, on a scene-to-scene basis, are very important for continuity, dramatic emphasis, and fluidity of movement, and are all decisions the layout artist makes.

1. A line design of the background is created.

2. Next, tones and shading are used to fill in and give the background layout more body.

3. In some cases, where time and budgets permit, the background sketch is colored.

4. Here, the layout artist checks the background for size correlation, match lines, color keying, and the path of action with proposed characters.

As the atmosphere or mood of the layout is created, lighting is worked out, too. The layout artist considers the time of day that the story takes place and shades the artwork accordingly. Lighting, along with colors, plays an important part in setting a mood. For key scenes where mood and location have changed, the layout artist makes a color-key (a rough comprehensive that includes the character in color to give a clear indication of what will be seen on the screen). This color comprehensive is valuable to both the background artist and the character designer who may be responsible for selecting the final colors for the characters. In an animated film, lighting functions similarly to theatrical lighting; the principal character is often highlighted to direct the audience's attention to the central action.

This artist is also responsible for designing the area in which the characters "act." A good sense of what is "real" in a particular setting combined with imagination are two significant qualities that are characteristic of good layout people. For an excellent example of why these sensitivities are so important, picture the inside of Gepetto's workshop in Disney's PINNOCHIO. The materials of the walls and floor, the furniture, the wooden clocks, and the workbench with its tools are imaginatively and authentically drawn to reflect the location and period depicted.

5. A path of action is sketched for the two characters in the leapfrog sequence. This step is used in setting up extremes for characters to be used by the key animator.

The layout artist also very roughly establishes the character's path of action to make sure that the background will effectively complement it. This action, drawn in a series of key positions, is used by the animator along with the field sizes the character will move within. When the layout is done, it's punched for registration with the peg bars on the animation stand and labeled with the title of the film, the sequence, and the scene numbers. Copies are then handed to the animators and the background artists.

The Background Artist

The background artist is responsible for creating the color mood of the film. This person works closely with the layout artist, using the color comprehensives for reference to create scenes that reflect and complement the action. Many backgrounds are now done in watercolor. It's an ideal medium for animation because the transparent quality contrasts with the opaqueness of the characters on the cels. At the same time, the watercolor complements the characters because there are no hard lines to conflict with the characters. The colors blend into each other creating a soft texture and an understated effect that the clearly delineated characters stand out on. A background is, after all, a complement to the action and must never detract from it. Background surfaces should be matte (nonglare) with a fine-grain surface. Illustration board or Arches' watercolor paper is often used in 16-lb weight for the background and 8-lb weight for the overlay.

Where a three-dimensional look is wanted, careful color planning is very important. For example, light color in the back and middle ground that blends with darker, warmer colors in the foreground creates an illusion of depth. To get a special effect, a background artist might use gouache, an air brush, marking pen, colored pencil, pen and ink, crayon, or whatever is needed.

Gouache is often used to darken areas or to add highlights because it applies well over watercolors. For those of you not acquainted with it, gouache is an opaque, somewhat thicker type of water-soluble pigment sometimes called designer's color. Since it does not have the translucency of water color, but is compatible with it, gouache is the ideal medium for very lights and very darks in background work. Air brushing creates yet another effect. It is excellent for highlighting and is often used in commercial films where mechanical parts require a look of hardness, precision, and realism. Where a good line is essential, a marking pen, pen and ink, pencil, and crayon are used. Any of these media or combinations are fine, providing the line will not easily rub off with handling, fade under strong camera lights, or disintegrate when blown up to full-screen size, where minor flaws will become major errors.

6. Working from the layout sketch, the background artist will paint the completed background, using directions from the layout artist.

The Key Animator

In the early days of animation, the artists worked straight through. That is, there were no distinctions according to the type of animation being done. An individual would be assigned a number of scenes and would complete them. Now the work is usually divided between the key animator, who draws the key points of movement for each character, and the in-betweener, who fills in the movement by drawing the action between these points.

The key animator works directly from the exposure sheet that indicates the scene transitions, pans, zooms, and other information the layout artist establishes, as well as the layout artist's rough plan of action and background rough. This artist must have a strong feeling for continuity to establish the key points of movement for a sequence and must be creative enough to convey as much expression as possible in the bodies and faces of the characters he or she draws. When the key points of movement are established, the work is passed to the in-betweener for the next step.

7. The exposure sheet is a visual display of the action to be filmed. It shows field sizes, character movements, pans, and every movement for the animation sequence. It is used by the key animator and ultimately created for the cameraman as a blueprint. This chart has all the moves, effects to be filmed, and accounts for every single frame in the picture.

8. The key animator draws extremes of each character in all the scenes and sequences assigned and prepares them for the in-betweener.

116

The In-Betweener

This animator carefully studies the key points in movement established by the key animator and draws the smooth, continuous movement of the character between these points. As the in-betweener works, the art is constantly checked by a method mentioned in Part Two, called the "flipping" technique in which the sheets are held with one hand and flipped by the thumb and index finger of the other hand. This technique gives the in-betweener an idea of how the character motion will look.

It is at this stage that a beginning animator learns all the rules governing the movement of animated figures. The in-betweener knows the different types of movement the characters make, including the "strut," "run," "skip," and "gallop." He or she also knows how clothes move with the body, and the difference between the movement of bodies and ordinarily inanimate objects. The in-betweener addresses numerous questions. Will gravity play a role? How do cloth and hair move when a character moves in various ways? What rules apply to animation that extend beyond physical law? To find out whether prospective students were aware of all of the above subtleties, Disney used to give them a test that required them to draw a bouncing ball. To pass the test, the would-be animator had to draw the action as follows: As the ball falls, its speed increases and the drawings are spaced further apart. Just before the ball hits the floor, it stretches slightly. When it hits the floor, it starts squashing and flattens out to a point of exaggeration. On the bounce, the ball starts to stretch again and moves rather fast, requiring fewer drawings. At the ball's highest point, it slows down, the drawings are spaced closer together and the ball resumes its natural shape. At least two bounces were required for the Disney test to illustrate the complete action.

An in-betweener must also master the lip-syncing technique and the drawing of characters in various perspectives. To fully appreciate the in-betweener's talents, visualize Disney's famous Pluto. As he walks, his tail is wagging, his body is moving, his nose is sniffing, and his eyes are moving. All of these movements require a special expertise that the in-betweener has to learn.

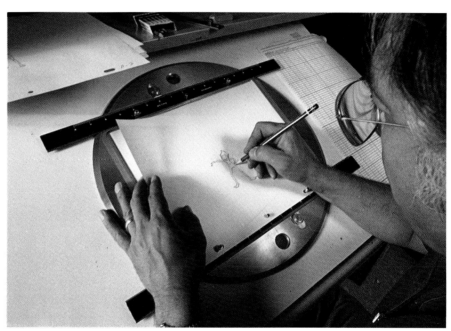

9. The in-betweener fills in the extremes with all the action required of the characters in the scene or sequence. Then, a "flipping" (or "flicking") technique is used in which the sheets are flipped in sequence with the thumb to check the smoothness of motion in an animated sequence.

The Clean-up Artist

The responsibility of the clean-up artist is to draw the completed character. This stage is done on a back-lighted table; the rough is placed over the lighted area and a new sheet of paper is taped over the rough to trace the character. Clean-up work is arduous and requires a skilled hand to maintain all the movement and vitality of the original line, in addition to refining expressions for a finished look. It is the clean-up artist's job to add the final touches to the character. Look at the rough and cleanup shown on pages 50 and 51 for a comparison of these two stages.

The most important responsibility of an inker is not only to maintain the accuracy of the line (badly traced lines tend to "animate" on their own), but also to retain the personality of the line peculiar to the animator who drew the character. The inker must faithfully reproduce the original lines with all the whimsy and lyricism of the original. To do this, he or she utilizes anything from Rapido-graph pens, crowquills, and brushes to wax pencils, paint lines, or self-lines. A self-line is a line inked with the same color as the opaquing color. It's often used for clouds or waves when a clearly defined dark outline is not desired.

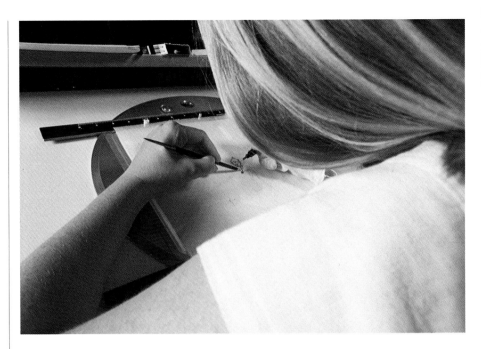

The Inker and Electrostatist

Though many fine inkers or tracers have had their responsibilities reduced with the introduction of the electrostatic method of copying cels from clean-up sheets, there are still exceptions that require the careful hand of these craftsmen. Large black areas, for example, cannot be copied electrostatically because excessive heat is conducted by the denser areas and the cel tends to warp. FELIX THE CAT could probably not be done on an electrostatic copying machine unless it was done in outline and painted in later. Similarly, THE PINK PANTHER cannot be done electrostatically because it requires a pink outline and the available color toner (powdered ink) is too transparent.

10. Inking the cels is done when the cleanup stage is complete. Although the development of the electrostatic copying technique has cut down the need for hand inking, it is still necessary in cases where there are solid dark areas of color.

Because acetate tends to pick up fingerprints very easily (and show them just as easily) the inker always wears gloves. The gloves usually have the thumb and first two fingers cut off to make holding the inking instrument easier. The glove also allows the inker's hand to move smoothly and freely over the cel. When the inking is completed and the ink is dry, the cels are ready to be opaqued.

The Opaquer or Colorist

Opaquing the cels for an entire film is very time-consuming. Most animators plan on two frames of film for every cel. Accordingly, an opaquer colors an average of twelve cels for every second of film. If any cel layering is used, the number is even higher.

Cels or acetates are opaqued on the reverse side of the inked or electrostated lines. Following the color models decided on by the layout and background artists, the opaquer chooses the right color tone. Special color shading is necessary for characters that aren't on the top cel layer or are executed on more than one layer, because each layer of acetate darkens the color on the cels beneath it. The paint is mixed according to the level on which it will be used; the deeper the cel, the lighter the color. The actual work is done over a light box to make sure the painting is even and consistent.

When the work is done, the cels are stacked separately to dry, inspected for mistakes, and cleaned very carefully over a black card that shows the dirt. The opaquer then cleans the cels with a soft cloth, moving from left to right. This left-to-right motion is important because vertical scratches reflect light much more than horizontal ones. When this step is complete, the clean cels are ready for the checker.

11. Opaquers or painters spend a great deal of time on the cels and must be careful to keep them clean. Coloring is done on the back side of the cel on the opposite side of the black art line.

The Checker

The checker is responsible for making certain that the cel work is camera-ready in every way. He or she uses an animation disc with a peg bar registration that matches the animation stand and refers to the exposure sheet, exactly as the cameraman will do. But instead of shooting, the checker looks for mistakes. Each cel is placed over the background it will be shot on and camera moves are simulated to make sure everything works correctly. The cels are checked for painting mistakes, dirt, and broken lines. The checking phase is very important to the production and must be done meticulously because reshooting after a mistake has been caught on screen is a very expensive process and causes unwanted time delays as well.

12. The checker places each cel on the background and checks the quality of art and all movement. Each cel is filmed one or two frames at a time using the platen to hold it down and keep cel shadows from being filmed.

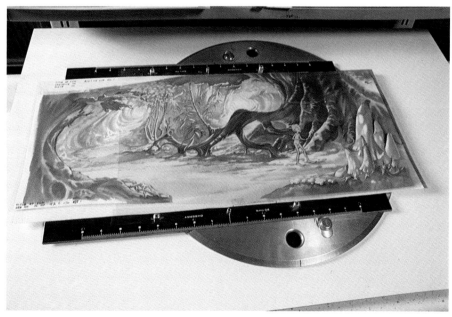

The Cameraman

The cameraman is responsible for quality photography of all the work performed by the artists on the production. Using the exposure sheet as a blueprint, this individual builds the completed film footage, frame by frame, on an animation stand. The animation stand is the cameraman's tool and he or she must have complete knowledge of the stand to achieve the best possible results.

Along with being a good photographer, the cameraman must know how to maintain the equipment used and have a state-of-the-art knowledge of what equipment is available to help make the job easier and faster. It is also this individual's responsibility to know and understand film stocks and their availability, to establish relationships with laboratory personnel, and to get the exposed film processed and workprinted so that the producer and director can see and evaluate the footage as soon as possible.

The Editor

After the film is shot and viewed by the producer, director, and all others who require a viewing, it is the editor's job to carefully make a final check of all the film footage for smooth movement, even after the checker has gone through the art. The next step is to add the sound-track. As the editor adds the music and sound effects, the overall results are measured for correct positioning. Animation editors should be experts at evaluating animation for movement, flow, and continuity. Often, action can be improved by the right adjustment of music or sound effects and an editor may often come up with an extra creative effect that will add to the film's quality.

13. The exposure sheet is a blueprint of the film. The cameraman uses it for frame-by-frame direction.

The Production Manager

The production manager is in charge of the purchasing of supplies in all stages of the film's production. It is the production manager who keeps supplies of paint in stock for the painters or opaquers, takes the cameraman's order for film stock, and replenishes all other supplies during the production.

Because the production manager is very familiar with the material supplies needed to make a film, he or she also helps the producer with the production's budget and often handles the fiscal management of the production when the studio is too small to have an accounting department.

Although the major responsibilities of each craftsman have been outlined, remember that there are no hard-and-fast rules for who handles what in an average studio. If the studio happens to be in a large metropolitan area where union regulations exist, then craftsmen will probably have clearly outlined responsibilities. In areas where there is no union, the studios are generally smaller and the animators "wear many hats."

PART EIGHT

Prominent Studios and Citizens in the World of Animation

The following introduction to prominent studios and citizens in the world of animation is by no means complete; such a wrap-up would fill several books of this size. This section is only intended to give you a general idea of the types of studios and craftsmen active in the field of animation today.

Walt Disney Productions

The half century that has elapsed since Walt Disney and his wife created their famous Mickey Mouse makes Walt Disney Productions the oldest and certainly the best-known animation studio in the world. Since Mickey's early days, audiences have enjoyed the tremendously creative output of this studio in numerous full-length films, including SNOW WHITE AND THE SEVEN DWARFS, PINOCCHIO, PETER PAN, FANTASIA, and more recently, THE JUNGLE BOOK, THE RESCUERS, and PETE'S DRAGON (a combination of live action and animation). Today, the Disney studio is still committed to very high quality, having proven that quality is the guarantee of profits and success.

Walt Disney (1901-1966)

Mickey Mouse, one of Disney's greatest "personalities," is shown as he appeared in various stages of his career. (© Walt Disney Productions)

While most other studios have done away with the pencil test, Disney animators continue to carefully look at every move prior to completion. The studio still has the largest assortment of colors, the most elaborately created background art, and a staff that is recognized for superior talent and creativity. The last nine original animators are about to retire and there is much talk around the studio about the new generation of animators now in apprenticeship. We will see their talents in the new Disney fantasy THE BLACK CAULDRON, due for release around 1984.

Breaking In:
Although the studio is not beating the bushes for artist applicants, it does keep an eye out for talent. What it takes to make it at the Disney Studio is outlined below:

A deep interest in the art of character animation.

A desire to make animated cartoons in the Disney fashion . . . with the Disney look.

The ability to apply thoughts and ideas to the art.

Moreover, an applicant to the Disney studio should know the studio's idea of what makes a good animator: An animator must be able to create real-life as well as exaggerated drawings. He or she must also understand and possess acting ability. This second requirement is an interesting one, because many who write about animation recognize this type of artist as one who has the ability to "act" or convey human emotions through his or her characters.

The studio is associated with the California Institute of the Arts which has a course in Disney-style animation given by Disney staff members. As in most institutions, scholarships are available in limited numbers. Address inquiries to:

Office of Admissions
California Institute of the Arts
24700 McBean Parkway
Valencia, California 91355
Attention: Jack Hannah

Openings at the Disney Studio are not limited to character animators; artists skilled in the fine arts can also make a signifi-cant contribution. Story writers, researchers, designers, story sketchers, layout and background designers and painters are all essential to the studio work which includes the production of high-quality features in both live action and animation. Bring a portfolio containing your samples. Generally, the ability to produce quick, rough sketches that show a good comprehension of life drawing and depict motion and a flair for caricature is essential. Layout portfolios should contain samples showing a real understanding of composition, perspective and design. Background paintings should be in watercolor or tempera medium showing attention to detail, atmosphere, and mood.

One of the things the Walt Disney studio is best known for is the continuity of design from scene to scene. The effect is that the film appears to have been done by one mind and hand, and not the reality . . . a team of artists with varying backgrounds. This effect is achieved as a result of the careful selection of talent and because most of the people at this studio have worked together for many years. It is the Disney look: the flawless execution of animation art and background that complements every motion planned. It all adds up to what could be appropriately termed as the "Disney gestalt." Animators who want to work as part of this system must plan to, if accepted, apply their talent for extended periods of time, perhaps their entire careers, to the pursuit of a style recognized all over the world.

For more information on the studio and the operations of Walt Disney Productions, the serious applicant can write to:

Walt Disney Productions
Animation Department
500 S. Buena Vista Street
Burbank, California 91521

This color sketch from Walt Disney's forthcoming animated feature film,
THE FOX AND THE HOUND, shows a realistic representation of animals reminiscent
of the earlier film BAMBI. (© Walt Disney Productions)

PINOCCHIO, the quintessence of character development in animation and perhaps
Walt Disney's greatest story feature, was released in 1940 at a production
cost of $2,600,000. (© Walt Disney Productions)

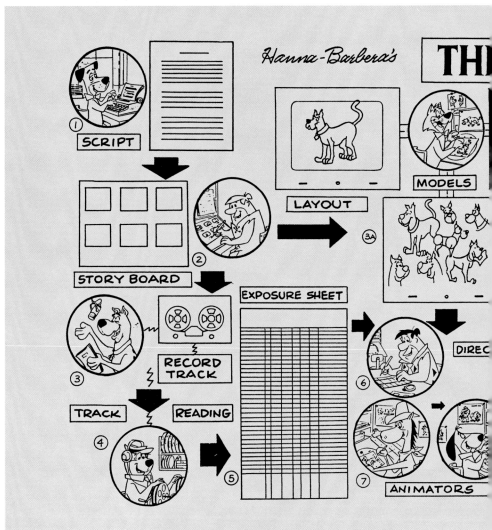

William Hanna (above) and Joseph Barbera founded Hanna-Barbera Productions 21 years ago and are currently the world's largest producers of cartoons for network television.

Hanna-Barbera Productions

William Hanna and Joseph Barbera, who are now high-level executives in one of the largest animation studios in the world, were also teamed together earlier in their careers at the drawing boards in the MGM studio. They were the brilliant and exceptionally gifted team that created MGM's TOM AND JERRY theatrical series. The series won seven academy awards and has since become a classic. Many of the shorts are still broadcast on television and of course carry the William Hanna and Joseph Barbera director's credits.

The first short introducing the Tom and Jerry characters was produced by Rudolf Ising in 1941. It was called PUSS GETS THE BOOT and was the first film the team of Hanna and Barbera worked on. Prior to that, Bill Hanna directed CAPTAIN AND THE KIDS cartoons for MGM and Joe Barbera was a story man with the independent Van Buren studio in New York. In 1957, Bill Hanna and Joe Barbera had been promoted to production heads of MGM when a major change occurred. The policies between distributors and exhibitors were changing and creating problems for studios promoting theatrical short films. In addition,

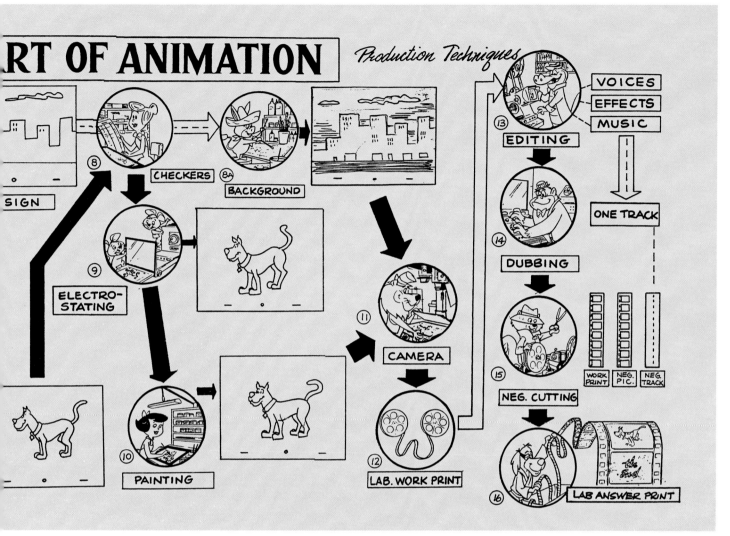

RT OF ANIMATION
Production Techniques

SIGN

(8) CHECKERS

(8A) BACKGROUND

(9) ELECTRO-STATING

(10) PAINTING

(11) CAMERA

(12) LAB. WORK PRINT

(13) EDITING

VOICES
EFFECTS
MUSIC

ONE TRACK

(14) DUBBING

(15) NEG. CUTTING

WORK PRINT | NEG. PIC. | NEG. TRACK

(16) LAB ANSWER PRINT

The stages of production for producing an animated film, showing the famous Hanna-Barbera characters.

television was competing for the weekly theatre audience and winning. Almost all of the theatrical animation studios ended production of cartoon shorts and hundreds of skilled animators were out of work. A few of them, such as Jack Zander who was with the TOM AND JERRY team at MGM, began doing commercial animation for television. Zander now runs a very busy commercial production house which he calls Zander's Animation Parlour. But Bill Hanna and Joe Barbera had other plans. Although the executives at MGM did not visualize the continuing profit of animated cartoons for television, Bill Hanna

and Joe Barbera could. They left MGM and independently created a show called RUFF AND REDDY.

Since their first independent venture, this studio has had numerous successful series, including such characters as Yogi Bear, Quick Draw McGraw, Huckleberry Hound, and the Flintstones. Though Hanna-Barbera was not the first studio to put limited motion animation on television, it was the first to do so successfully on a continuing basis. The studio has produced this type of animation for television for more than 20 years. It is particularly popular as entertain-

ment for children on Saturday mornings in the United States. Accordingly, this popularity created the term "kiddie video" or KidVid.

Hanna-Barbera, along with most others in the industry, is also producing full animation films. CHARLOTTE'S WEB, a feature length film released in 1972, was fully animated, as is the forthcoming Hanna-Barbera production HEIDI'S SONG.

Breaking In:

Because of its size and production needs, Hanna-Barbera keeps an animation class going on a fairly constant basis. An animation applicant to Hanna-Barbera should have the same qualifications as an entry-level applicant to the Disney studio. If an applicant qualifies, the classes at Hanna-Barbera are provided tuition-free.

In charge of the class at Hanna-Barbera is a man who has animated or directed at almost every major animation studio in the business. His name is Harry Love. Some of the well-known characters Love has worked on are Porky Pig and Bugs Bunny. He started at the old Harrison and Gould studio in New York in the 1920s and has had his elbows on the boards of the Charles Mintz studio, Warner Brothers, Walt Disney Productions, and DePatie-Freleng prior to moving to Hanna-Barbera.

Love says the scope of animation styles and techniques at Hanna-Barbera is so wide that if an applicant can draw well, he or she has a good chance. He thinks the same way Don Duckwall of Walt Disney Productions does: **the ability to draw life forms in motion, loosely but well formed, and quickly, from various angles is most important.** Love adds, "demonstrating a good knowledge of anatomy is important, quickly rendered with a strong line of action."

As a final note, Love says, "Bring only your talent and your ambition." If an applicant is accepted at Hanna-Barbera, there are free continuous classes, pencils, paper, and coffee. For further information, write:

Harry Love
Supervisor, Animation
 Training Program
Hanna-Barbera Productions
3400 Cahuenga Boulevard
Hollywood, California 90068

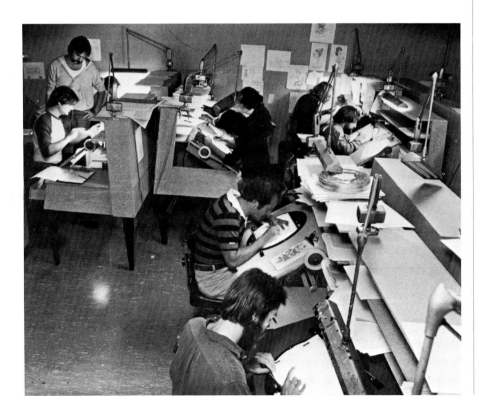

The Hanna-Barbera animation classes are set up to reflect actual working conditions. The better students are selected for positions with the studio as vacancies occur. Here, we see part of a class at work receiving individual instruction.

DePatie-Freleng Enterprises

In all industries, new organizations spring up from older ones. As mentioned earlier, Hanna-Barbera Productions was formed by two MGM directors. Similarly, the Warner Brothers animation department was formed from the older Schlesinger studio. When Warner's stopped producing theatrical shorts, a major unit director, Isadore (Friz) Freleng, left to create a separate studio and partnership with DePatie, who was a studio executive with Warner Brothers at the time. Friz Freleng's background reflects the high level of expertise and experience he brought to his new partnership with DePatie. Earlier in his career he worked at the Film Ad Company in Kansas City, around 1924, where other talents such as Walt Disney, Ub Iwerks, Hugh Harman, and Rudolph Ising got experience. Disney had just left for California to start his own studio when Freleng arrived.

Freleng left the Film Ad Company to work for Disney for a time and then decided to go back to Kansas City. Later, he went to New York and worked with Charles Mintz animating the KRAZY KAT series.

DePatie-Freleng's characters show the effect of stylization and economy of design used today.

Probably the most pivotal point in Freleng's career was his move to Leon Schlesinger's studio about the time Schlesinger joined Warner Brothers. It was at Warner Brothers that Freleng began producing the outstanding theatrical shorts that would become classics. Freleng had the longest tenure at Warner Brothers, from 1932 to 1964, during which he directed 249 theatrical shorts. He introduced the brilliantly created characters of Porky Pig, Sylvester, Yosemite Sam, and Tweetie Pie. In fact, he won the first Academy Award for Warner's with Tweetie Pie, released in 1947.

The DePatie-Freleng studio produces numerous types of animation. One is the theatrical short which is fully animated, and runs about 6½ minutes. Shorts are released by United Artists and distributed throughout the world. The most popular is THE PINK PANTHER series. The shorts are also packaged into half-hour formats and leased to network television.

Another type of animation produced at the DePatie-Freleng studio is the limited-motion animation used for children's cartoons. Like most of the KidVid shows, it depends less on refined character animation and more on the use of dialogue and situations. These productions are done in this way primarily because of time and economic limitations. For example,

These characters, many of which were designed and developed at the old Warner Brothers studio by Isadore "Fritz" Freleng, exemplify the genuine appeal of cel animated "personalities." (© Warner Brothers Inc. All rights reserved.)

"SYLVESTER"

YOSEMITE SAM

"TWEETY"

the Warner Brothers cartoon studio with a crew of 60 to 70 people produced approximately three hours of film per year. Using limited-motion animation, DePatie-Freleng produces about four times as much screen time per person in a year.

The studio also does television commercials and, though infrequent, half-hour specials for television, such as DR. SEUSS, THE PINK PANTHER, and the ABC AFTERSCHOOL SPECIALS.

Friz Freleng sees DePatie-Freleng moving into feature animation and looks forward to a time when he thinks television networks will purchase and schedule even more quality animation for prime-time broadcast.

Breaking In:
DePatie-Freleng always looks for professional talent, but does not have an animation school.

Isadore "Friz" Freleng, the dean of Warner Brothers' animators, started with Walt Disney at the Hyperion Avenue studio. Moving to Warner's after serving with Charles Mintz, he created, among others, Porky Pig and Tweetie Pie. He is now Executive Producer and the Executive Vice President of DePatie-Freleng of Pink Panther fame.

Filmation Studios

Attesting to the old adage "where there's a will, there's a way" are two bright businessmen from the east coast of the United States, Lou Scheimer and Norm Prescott, who manage Filmation Studios. Neither has an animation background. Lou Scheimer attended the Carnegie Institute of Technology, and founded the Filmation Studios in 1962. Norm Prescott has a background in broadcasting and has also held positions at Embassy Pictures Corporation and Belvision (a Belgium animation production and publishing company). While at Belvision, he co-produced the film PINOCCHIO IN OUTER SPACE which enjoyed a successful release in the U.S. and Japan.

In 1965, Prescott joined Lou Scheimer at Filmation, and they quickly secured the rights to use SUPERMAN in a very successful adventure series that ran 52 episodes. SUPERBOY, a spin-off of SUPERMAN, extended the series an additional 26 episodes. Producing more than 500 half-hour segments since it began, Filmation has been a powerhouse in the limited motion field for KidVid. The studio has made some very wise business choices and garnered considerable critical acclaim for shows such as STAR TREK and FAT ALBERT. Their ARCHIE series has run for eight years and holds the record for the longest running animated children's program. The studio has a reputation for successfully adapting numerous live action shows to limited motion animation, including Tarzan, Batman, Star Trek, and the New Adventures of Gilligan.

©1978 King Features Syndicate, Inc.

Filmation studios is a powerhouse for children's programming on Saturday morning television. (Top) Two prehistoric animals in a scene from Flash Gordon (Courtesy of King Features Syndicate). (Above) The popular Archie Series.

Breaking In:
The Filmation Studio is very large, with more than 400 employees. Although it does not have a school, a young professional with talent has a fairly good chance of breaking in, depending on the production requirements at the time of application. For more information on either the studio or employment, write:

Filmation Studios
18107 Sherman Way
Reseda, California 91335

Chuck Jones Enterprises

Chuck Jones is perhaps the most widely known animator outside of Walt Disney. This is not by power of his creative energy alone. He is also an articulate, erudite man with an easy smile who possesses a tremendous amount of enthusiasm for the creative projects he pursues.

After graduating from the Chouinard Art School, Jones started with Ub Iwerks' studio in Hollywood where he worked on the FLIP THE FROG series. Jones had just left the Disney Studio for a ten-year solo stint. He tried several other studios, returned to Iwerks' studio, and then made a move to the Schlesinger studio, in the late thirties, where Fritz Freleng was then working.

By the time the studio was bought by Warner Brothers, Jones was directing. While with Warner Brothers, he apprenticed under Tex Avery in an old building known as "Termite Terrace." At this time, the studio created the famous Bugs Bunny and Daffy Duck. Later, Jones originated such famed cartoon characters as the Roadrunner, Wile E. Coyote, and Pepe Le Pew. Among his impressive credits are ONE FROGGY EVENING, starring Michigan J. the singing frog (released in 1956), and two years later, WHAT'S OPERA DOC?

With the demise of the Warner Brothers studio in 1964, Jones independently went on to win many awards and critical acclaim producing television specials such as Dr. Seuss' HOW THE GRINCH STOLE CHRISTMAS, THE CAT IN THE HAT, and THE POGO BIRTHDAY SPECIAL.

Now heading his own production company, Chuck Jones produces fully animated specials primarily for prime-time television. In 1973, as executive producer on Richard William's A CHRISTMAS CAROL, he helped produce a classic which has run every Christmas since its release. His studio has more recently worked on several projects, among which is a RAGGEDY ANN AND ANDY SPECIAL for Christmas, released 1978.

Jones lectures extensively at colleges, universities, and film festivals throughout the United States and overseas. Like Disney, his work is timeless and is enjoyed by audiences throughout the world.

Breaking In:
The Chuck Jones Enterprises studio, located in a modern high-rise building in Hollywood, is a small creative shop that caters to specialized projects. While there may be a job or two for beginning artists, the studio usually employs only highly skilled, experienced professionals.

Chuck Jones, animation writer, director, producer, and artist, has according to TIME Magazine, "made moviegoers laugh as often and as well as Chaplin or Keaton." A three-time Academy Award and Peabody Award winner, he now manages his own studio, Chuck Jones Enterprises, in Hollywood.

Richard Williams
Animation Limited

Richard Williams runs two completely operational studios; one is his mainstay in London, the other is located in Hollywood. In Hollywood, he is slowly putting together his long-awaited THE THIEF AND THE COBBLER in addition to creating award-winning television commercials. Williams is an outstanding example of an artist who works for others in order to have money for personal projects, and he does both well.

Williams was born in Toronto in 1933, the year the Disney Studio released THE THREE LITTLE PIGS. Like many of today's animators, he was impressed as a child by the extraordinary films Disney produced. He remembers being particularly fascinated by SNOW WHITE. Even at that early age, he was already drawing and decided that it would be his life ambition. He also recalls touring the Disney studio at the age of eighteen, while the studio was working on ALICE IN WONDERLAND. At that time, he was told to continue learning to draw.

Williams learned to draw well and pursued his interest in animation. He worked for a gifted British animator, George Dunning, doing animation for television commercials while continuing work on his own film, THE LITTLE ISLAND. This first independent film, released in 1958, won him numerous awards and provided a vital impetus to continue his creativity. Since then, Richard Williams has won awards almost every year for commercial work such as his famous VOLKSWAGEN BEETLEKILLER. In 1972, he became the first British animator to win an Academy Award for animation with his version of Charles Dickens' A CHRISTMAS CAROL.

"Good, Truth and Beauty," the characters from Richard Williams' award-winning film THE LITTLE ISLAND. In addition to winning the Grand Prix at the Venice International Shorts and Documentary Festival and the British Film Academy Award, both in 1958, THE LITTLE ISLAND has won awards at festivals in West Germany, Vienna, Trieste, and Vancouver.

King Charles II, in London, looks down quietly at an animated Richard Williams. This picture perhaps best describes Williams' busy schedule while maintaining both a London and Hollywood studio.

From Richard Williams' forthcoming animated feature film THE THIEF AND THE COBBLER. The Cobbler shyly puts a repaired slipper on Princess Yum-Yum's foot.

Williams has also done many film titles and opening sequences for feature films such as WHAT'S NEW PUSSYCAT?, THE GRADUATE, CASINO ROYALE, and THE RETURN OF THE PINK PANTHER. His very best title sequence, also used in transitions during the film, was for THE CHARGE OF THE LIGHT BRIGADE.

The quality of Williams' work is readily apparent in the flowing and detailed style of the characters in his feature-length animated film RAGGEDY ANN AND ANDY, released in 1977. He is currently applying his talents to his forthcoming film, THE THIEF AND THE COBBLER, financed by the profits from his commercial work to ensure that he has complete creative freedom. He has been working on this special project for several years and hopes to complete it in the near future.

Breaking In:
As in the case of Chuck Jones Enterprises, the Richard Williams animation studio is small and highly creative—almost a personal extension of Williams' taste, demanding only highly skilled and gifted professionals. He does hire young people, however, if they have what it takes.

Kurtz & Friends

One of the best known and certainly the most-successful animation studios for television commercials is Kurtz & Friends in Hollywood, California. Hooper White, a top advertising professional and nationally known consultant, has made the following observation of this creative studio in an issue of ADVERTISING AGE: "From a courtyard of a 1920s white frame building right out of early Hollywood comes some of the most refreshing animation seen on television."

Bob Kurtz is head friend, ably supported by Bob Peluce, a most talented designer of animation, and a staff of imaginative young people well managed by producer Loraine Roberts. Kurtz & Friends has collected numerous commercial awards including Clios and the AAW Sweepstakes on the West Coast. Its 1978 Clio winner, mentioned in Part Two, is a fine example of metamorphic animation for the Chevron Oil Co. Called "STAFF OF LIFE," the animation describes how Chevron divides its loaf of money, slice by slice. The company makes a metamorphic change into a friendly looking dinosaur who eats the slices as the division of money is explained.

Bob Kurtz, a Disney alumnus, is probably aptly placed into the third generation of animators of Hollywood. After graduating from the same art school that Chuck Jones attended (Chouinard), he went to the Disney studio. A few years later he left Disney and joined a well-known animation house called FilmFair. After gaining three years of experience doing television commercials for Film-

Bob Kurtz, third generation Hollywood animator, puts on his real face when he gets behind the drawing board.

Two animated commercials by Kurtz & Friends: (above) ETHEL AND THE KIDS from a spot created for Heinz and (left) MOVING FOOD for Reynolds Aluminum.

Fair, Kurtz decided to start his own company in 1971. Kurtz has been very successful, primarily because of his willingness to try new approaches to animation. One of his maxims is "Anything . . . any **thing**, or any artist's style, can be moved on film." He feels the only limitation is in an animator's mind.

While many of the animation houses working on television commercials take over after an ad agency has come up with concept and storyboard, Kurtz & Friends is primarily a total concept house and, like the early commercial animators, takes on a project from the very beginning most of the time. Spots they produce are usually conceived, storyboarded and produced by the Kurtz & Friends studio.

Bob Kurtz believes that the animation business is still free. He states, "Anyone can show a reel and the buyer either likes it or he doesn't. With live action, there may be a lot of game playing, but not with animation. You're not wheeling and dealing; you're just showing your stuff." He comments further, "Commercials afford creativity, but there's also a tremendous amount of pressure associated with them in terms of time, delivery, and profession-alism. But you also have to have the liberty to experiment because there is an important audience out there. That audience has to be stimulated and animation is a good way to do that."

MORE THAN A NAME, a 30-second spot for Ariens Company, a manufacturer of garden equipment, shows the typical Kurtz & Friends style—a free flowing design unlimited by time and space.

PART NINE

Films to Use

At this point you should be pretty familiar with the time and effort in producing an animated film. So make sure that your investment pays off by choosing the right film for your needs. Since there are dozens of Kodak films available, we've narrowed the list down to those that work best for animation. The choices discussed below include only color films because they're more popular, but there are several black-and-white films listed in the chart for those who prefer it.

Obviously, your camera will determine what your film format will be. If you're just starting out and working with a super 8 movie camera, try the KODAK EKTACHROME Reversal Films, such as KODAK EKTACHROME EF Film 7242 (Tungsten), EKTACHROME 160 Movie Film (Type A), and EKTACHROME 160 Movie Film (Type G). Probably the best choice among these three is the EKTACHROME 160 (Type A) Film because this film has the best color balance for animation. Another film that you may want to consider is KODACHROME 40 Movie Film (Type A). This film is characterized by extremely fine grain and is sharper and more contrasty than the EKTACHROME 160 (Type A) Film. In fact, the KODACHROME 40 Movie Film is probably the best choice for super 8 film because the speed is better for animation than the other films. Processing for the KODACHROME 40 Movie Film may take a little longer than for EKTACHROME 160 Movie Film if it has to be sent to Kodak, but if you live in or near any large city, you can most likely have it done in a local lab.

For 16 mm films, you can choose between EASTMAN EKTACHROME Video News 7240 (Tungsten), EKTACHROME Commercial 7252, and EKTACHROME EF 7242 Reversal Films, KODACHROME Movie Film (Type A) 7270, and EASTMAN Color Negative II Film 7247. These films all work well for animation, depending on your release print needs. EKTACHROME 7240 and 7242 are more for situations where just an original or only a few prints are needed for projection. Also, both EKTACHROME Films are color-balanced for television broadcast, so if you are planning a production for television, and you don't need a large number of release prints, you may want to consider these two films. The EKTACHROME Films 7240 and 7242 are easy to work with because the result is a positive image that can be viewed and projected directly. EKTACHROME 7252 Commercial Film is recommended for an animator who makes films, such as commercials, that require a number of release prints. For all three EKTACHROME Films, a laboratory can produce reversal release prints from the original or produce an internegative from which prints can be made, if multiple copies of the film are desired. The latter method is most economical when more than a few prints are needed.

KODACHROME Movie Film 7270 is a good choice for animation because you'll be working in a controlled high light-level situation on an animation stand so you won't need the higher speeds of the other films. Like the EKTACHROME Films, the result is a positive image that can also be viewed and projected directly. And if you don't need copies, KODACHROME 7270 will render a fine-grain, high-quality original.

EASTMAN Color Negative II Film is used where special effects, titles, and a great number of release prints are used. But don't forget that your processed original will have negative images, which means that you'll need to have a work print made for evaluation, editing, and projection purposes. The above information on EKTACHROME and EASTMAN Color Negative Films should help you select the best film based on your specific needs, including the number of release prints you want. If there are still several similar films that you are considering, such as the EKTACHROME 7240 and 7242, make your final selection based on the availability of laboratory services. Most motion picture labs handle the EKTACHROME Films, but it's still a good idea to check on processing services before you make your decision. You should also do the same check before you decide to shoot on negative stock.

When you've selected the film that seems to meet your needs, do an exposure series on it to make sure you're getting the quality you want before you begin shooting an animation sequence. The best way to do this is to put a background or cel on the animation stand and try an exposure series. Take a light meter reading first and start at the f/stop that the meter indicates. Before you use any film, write the beginning f/stop on a card and place it somewhere near the edge of the piece you're filming. If the meter reads f/11, write "f/11 = N" on the card to indicate that it's the normal exposure according to your meter. You should also write down the film code number (such as 7242) on the card. Then try half-stop increments above and below your starting f/stop, using a card that indicates each stop you try. Run off ten to twenty seconds (or six to twelve feet) of film—enough to evaluate your chosen f/stop on the projection screen. Make sure your camera is not on "automatic" if it has an automatic exposure control. This exposure series will show you what exposure is right for your individual camera, film, and lighting conditions. Keep in mind that some cameras (especially spring-wound and amateur battery-powered cameras) don't run at full speed during single-frame exposure. Thus, if you want twelve frames of one cel at the end of a sequence, remember to continue with single-frame exposures, because the continuous run speed may have half the exposure of a single-frame exposure. Also, the spring-wound cameras (particularly the BOLEX H series) tend to give longer and longer exposures as the spring rewinds. So if you use a spring-wound camera, you'll need to rewind it fairly often.

The cels, lights, glass on the platen, and numerous other things reflect light on different areas of the compound, so your light meter may not give you a true reading. And while you're doing your exposure series you can also check the framing and alignment of the camera. Now is the time to become aware of any necessary adjustments.

Camera Films For Animation

Name of Film	Film Code No. 16 mm	Film Code No. Super 8	Type	Exposure Index	Use	Processing
Eastman Plus-X negative film	7231	—	Black-and-white Negative	64	Speed and grain characteristics make this film well suited for general motion picture projection.	Black-and-white with Developer D-96
Eastman Ektachrome video news film (Tungsten)	7240	—	Color Reversal	125	Suitable for television broadcast.	Commercial Labs, Process VNF-1 or RVNP.
Kodak Ektachrome EF film (tungsten)	7242	7242**	Color Reversal	125	Suitable for television broadcast.	Commercial Labs, Process ME-4
Eastman Color negative II film	7247*	—	Color Negative	100	Intended for general motion picture production.	Commercial Labs, Process ECN-2
Eastman Ektachrome commercial film	7252	—	Color Reversal	25	Provides low-contrast originals for color-release prints of good projection contrast.	Commercial Labs, Process ECO-3.
Kodak Plus-X reversal film	7276	7276	Black-and-white Reversal	40	Use with ample artificial illumination.	Commercial Labs. Kodak liquid reversal chemicals
Kodak Ektachrome 160 movie film (Type A)	—	7245	Color Reversal	160	Accommodates lower light levels and artificial lighting.	This film requires Process EM-25 or Kodak Ektachrome movie chemicals.
Kodak Type G Ektachrome 160 movie film	—	7248	Color Reversal	160	Accommodates lower light levels and artificial lighting. "No filter necessary" for Type G.	This film requires Process EM-25 or Kodak Ektachrome movie chemicals.
Kodachrome 40 movie film (Type A)	7270	7268**	Color Reversal	40	Has extremely high sharpness and fine grain.	This film requires Process K-14.
Eastman high contrast panchromatic film	5369 35 mm only	—	Black-and-white intermediate		A laboratory film used for traveling mattes and other special effects.	Black-and-white with Developer D-97

*Also available in 35 mm format with same characteristics (5247).
**Super 8 200-ft Film (61 m) cartridge also available.

NOTE: Because films are changed from time to time and new ones are introduced, check with your local Kodak dealer on the latest data if you use this book beyond a year of the printing date.

Once you've done your exposure series and have some film to be processed, there are a few important things you should know. If you've had film processed before, you already know these things; if not, here are a few points we'd like to pass on about choosing the best film laboratory for your needs.

During postproduction, you will be spending quite a bit of time and money with a film laboratory of your choice, so locating the "right" lab is extremely important. Ideally, you should have some "feeling" for a lab early in the production phase, before you have many hours worth of exposed film on your hands and are wondering what to do with it. How do you find that lab?

Generally, the lab that gets your business will be the one whose capabilities best match the requirements for your particular job. Every lab is different in terms of the technical services it offers, its attitude toward clients, its personnel, its track record on similar projects, its size and location, its price structure, and so on. You must weigh all of these factors against the job at hand to reach the proper choice.

Of course, nearly every production has different requirements. A production filmed in 35 mm for television distribution will most likely go to a different lab than a job shot in 16 mm for reduction to super 8 and used as point-of-purchase advertising in local stores. Your challenge as an efficient animator/producer is to find the lab that can satisfy the greatest number of your needs on schedule and within your budget. At best, you are faced with a number of trade-offs. For example, consider the question of big lab versus small lab.

The big lab usually offers more competitive pricing, more complete in-house capability, and excellent quality control. On the other hand, its bigness may result in your smaller job taking a back seat to "important" productions, in difficulty finding the person in charge of your job, and so forth.

The small lab, on the other hand, usually offers custom handling of your job and easy access to the right people for advice and counsel. But they may have to charge more to support their custom operation, may have to subcontract more of your job, and may not produce as high-quality an end product.

Look at the situation another way. Suppose you are a beginning animator aspiring to professional status. Your camera-original and release print footage will probably be less than that produced by the well-established professional. Also, it will very likely be less demanding technically (optical effects, complicated sound mixes, etc). It is even possible that you will need a bit more coaching than the long-time animator. Compromising a bit on the price to get the benefits a smaller lab could offer may be the right approach in this situation.

How about a lab's location? If you choose a lab that is a significant distance from your place of business (because it is well known or more price competitive), you will be faced with the potential hazards and increased costs of shipping valuable footage to and from the lab. Your daily communications with the lab will also be more difficult. Perhaps the smaller local lab would be a better choice in this case.

Obviously, the problem of choosing the right lab involves many variables and no pat answers. In the beginning, you will have to rely on information printed in comprehensive directories of motion picture services, the advice of your peers (very subjective, at best), and your own intuition (does the place feel right?). As you become more experienced through comparative shopping and experimentation, the task of choosing your lab will become easier. Once you have made your choice, get to know the personnel as well as possible and tell them as much as needed about yourself, your needs, and your style. The more they know about you and your production, the better they can serve you.

PART TEN

How to Find and Work With a Producer

Here's a section written for those of you who may prefer to buy the services of a producer, instead of producing your own film. The following suggestions should help you find and work effectively with an animation producer.

How to Find a Producer

Look first at your in-house services for references—a communications department, a public relations group, an audio-visual department. If you go to outside producers, ask other people who have commissioned animation work in the past. Perhaps they can suggest an animator with a good reputation.

Producer lists are available in directories, the Yellow Pages, and other sources. However, these lists are only a starting point. You need a creative communicator/problem-solver whose work you like, but you can't take time to look at samples from everyone. So, proceed as you would in selecting any unfamiliar service. Try to get recommendations from people whose needs are similar to yours, and ask the producers for lists of recent clients. Choosing by reputation and recommendations, narrow your list to three or four, and plan to look at **their** work. You may want to include one more who impresses you even if the references don't.

Then get in touch with your prospects. Tell them what you want to say and to whom, how much you want to spend, and that you want to see examples of their efforts. We suggest you look for creativity, quality, and practicality in their work, and reserve judgment on the technical accuracy of their statements and visuals. You are the subject expert, and you will be able to keep the facts straight.

How to Work With a Producer

1. Tell your producer what you want to accomplish. Put your objectives in writing.

   Your contributions are
   Your objectives
   Your subject knowledge
   Your knowledge of the audience
   (And of course) Your money

   Your producer's contributions are
   Imagination and creativity
   Production expertise and resources
   Desire to accomplish your objectives and make your film effective.

2. Tell your producer the mood you want to establish and the overall effect you want to achieve.

3. Tell the producer everything you can about your audience the age group, who they are and what they are like, what their interests are, and why they are going to be your audience.

4. Expect to pay a fair price. Remember, you are not paying for something you can do for nothing.

5. Agree on a reasonable deadline. You can't have it tomorrow. Period. Start with the due date and work out a schedule. Animation is very time-consuming.

6. Review the storyboards as soon as possible. Nothing will kill a producer's enthusiasm quicker than having to sit and wait.

7. Establish checkpoints. What must the producer deliver? When?

PART ELEVEN

Glossary of Technical Terms

Acetate (cellulose triacetate) A "support" material frequently used for motion picture film base. Also in sheet form for overlay cels.

Action The movement of the subject within the camera field of view. Also such movement as represented on film.

Aerial Image An image focused by a projection lens near a field or relay lens. A camera lens is then used to form a real image on the film from the aerial image. A cel or another material can be placed at the aerial-image location to combine it with the aerial image on film.

Anamorphic Lens Designed for wide-screen movie photography and projection. A lens that produces a "squeezed" image on film in the camera. When projected on a screen using an appropriate lens to reverse the effect, the image spreads out to lifelike proportions.

Animated Zoom A zoom effect achieved by making progressive changes in the sizes of artwork, rather than by moving the camera toward or away from the subject, in contrast with a continuous movement of the camera or a zoom accomplished by the adjustment of a variable focal-length lens.

Animation The technique of creating seemingly lifelike movement in normally inanimate objects or drawings through the medium of motion pictures. The term is also used for the sequence of drawings made to create that movement and for the movement itself when seen on the screen.

Animation Board A standard drawing board adapted for animation drawing by the addition of an animation disc or a registration peg-bar system. Also a name sometimes given to the top of the compound on an animation stand.

Animation Camera A motion picture camera with special capability for animation work, which usually includes frame and footage counters, the ability to expose a single frame at a time, reverse-filming capability, and parallax-free viewing.

Animation Stand A specially designed unit for holding and photographing artwork, which includes a camera, lighting equipment, registration device, platen, and compound table.

Answer Print The first combined picture and sound print, in release form, offered by the laboratory to the producer for acceptance. It is usually studied carefully to determine whether further changes are required prior to release printing. (UFPA*)

Aperture (1) Lens: The orifice, usually an adjustable iris, that limits the amount of light passing through a lens. (2) Camera: In motion picture cameras, the mask opening that defines the area of each frame exposed. (3) Projector: In motion picture projectors, the mask opening that defines the area of each frame projected.

Atmosphere Sketch The director's or layout artist's quick sketch used to create a specific mood for a scene. This sketch is then used in preparing the background of a scene.

Background (1) Artwork: The setting against (or over) which animation takes place. (2) Live Action: The character or objects appearing farthest from the camera.

Backlighting Light transmitted from beneath a drawing or a cel to produce a silhouette or to illuminate transparent colors applied to an acetate base.

Backward Take A technique in which the camera motor is placed in reverse drive and an image filmed. In scratch-off animation, for example, a line is inked on a cel, then removed bit by bit as it is filmed. The resulting image appears to grow when projected forward, as in a growing tree, footprints in the snow, or lines on a map.

Bar Sheet A frame-for-frame graph of words, major beats in the music, and sound effects recorded on the sound track; used to plan the movement of art and camera.

Beat The musical tempo (of the sound track) used for timing animation action.

Bipack Filming The running of two films simultaneously through a camera or printer, either to expose both or expose one through the other, using the one nearest to the lens as a mask. Often used to combine live action with animated images.

Blank A cel without a drawing, used in photography to keep the number of cel levels constant throughout a scene to avoid changes of background color.

Burn-In The photographic double exposure of a title or other subject matter over previously exposed film.

Cel A transparent sheet of cellulose acetate or similar plastic serving as a support or overlay for drawings, lettering, etc, in animation and title work. (To avoid possible confusion with biological "cells," the preferred spelling is with one "l.") Cels are usually punched to fit pegs on the artist's easel and/or the platen of the animation stand to help register successive cels during artwork and photography.

Cel Level The number of separate cels placed one over the other (over a common background) and photographed at the same time.

Checker The person who checks the camera-ready art (cels and background) just before filming for order, line and paint fallouts, completion, cleanliness, and continuity.

Clean-up Making finished layout drawings from roughs. Also, removing surplus ink, paint, fingerprints, and dust from cels before photography.

Close-up A detail photographed with a long focal-length lens, or from such a short distance that only a small portion of the subject fills a frame of film.

Color Correction Alteration of tonal values of colored objects or images by the use of light filters, either with camera or printer (UFPA). Often called color timing when done in a printer.

Color Model A specimen cel designed in conjunction with the background of each subject and painted in colors or tones as a guide to the painting of the whole scene. Also called color key.

Color Temperature The color quality—expressed in degrees Kelvin (K)—of the light source. The higher the color temperature, the bluer the light; the lower the temperature, the redder the light.

Composite A single piece of film bearing both picture and matching sound. The sound may be set up in any of the standard synchronous relationships to the picture. (UFA)

Composition The distribution, balance, and general relationship of masses and degrees of light and shade, line, and color within a picture area. (UFPA)

Compound The table portion of an animation stand that can be moved with great precision and on which the artwork is placed during photography.

Continuity An unbroken flow of events and styles from one scene to another.

Control Console The console, usually located beside an automated animation stand, that is used to control the movements of the animation stand compound and camera.

Credits Lines of acknowledgment for those persons responsible for the story, sets, direction, and so forth.

Cut (1) An instantaneous change from one scene to another—as if the last frame of one scene and the first frame of the following scene were spliced together. (2) A command used to stop operation of the camera, action, and/or sound recording equipment on a set. (3) To sever or splice film in the editing process. (UFPA)

Cutout A drawing or part of a drawing that is made on thin illustration board instead of cels. It can be placed on a background or used in combination with drawings on cels.

Cycle A series of animated drawings or cels, which can be photographed over and over to create the illusion of continuing, repeated action.

Dailies (Rushes) Usually a one-light print, made without regard to color balance, from which the action is checked and the best takes selected.

Definition The clarity or distinctness with which detail of an image is rendered; fidelity of reproduction of sound or image (UFPA*).

Density A convenient term used to express the light-stopping characteristic of the film, which is often described as "dark" or "light." The logarithm of the opacity of developed photographic film.

*With permission of the University Film Association

Depth of Field The distance between the nearest and farthest objects that will be recorded within acceptable limits of sharp focus on the film; must be considered especially in multiplane cel work and three-dimensional animation with backgrounds.

Dissolve An optical or camera effect in which one scene gradually fades out at the same time that a second scene fades in. There is an apparent double exposure during the center portion of a dissolve sequence where the two scenes overlap.

Dolly (1) A special truck built to carry a camera, or a camera and cameraman, to facilitate movement of the camera during the shooting of scenes. (2) To move the camera by means of a dolly while shooting a scene. (UFPA)

Double (Multiple) Exposure The photographic recording of two (or more) images on the same strip of film. The images may be either superimposed or side by side in any relationship, sometimes individually vignetted. (UFPA)

Drop Shadow A shadow line used behind titles to enhance their appearance and improve their legibility.

Dry Brush Technique The process in which a paint brush is dipped into paint, brushed on a practice cel until nearly dry, and then applied immediately on the cel to create a special effect such as a speed blur or tone gradation.

Dubbing The addition of sound (either music or dialogue) to a visual presentation via a rerecording process, which prepares a complete sound track (usually magnetic) that can be transferred to and synchronized with the visual presentation.

Editing The process of assembling, arranging, and trimming the desired scenes and sound tracks to create the final film.

Emulsion Speed The photosensitivity of an emulsion, usually expressed as an index number based on the film manufacturer's recommendations for the use of the film under typical conditions of exposure and development. (UFPA)

Exposure The process of subjecting a photographic film to any given intensity of light in such a manner that it will produce a latent image in the emulsion.

Exposure Meter An optical or photoelectrical device used to determine the amount of light falling on or reflected by a subject so that the film can be correctly exposed.

Exposure Sheet A guide that lists every frame of a film on a sequential basis indicating all compound and camera movements as the animation art is filmed. Used by the animation stand operator.

Extremes Drawings showing the animated subject at the critical moments of an action. Drawings of the intermediate phases of the action are subsequently produced by in-betweeners.

Fade Exposure of motion picture film either in the camera or during subsequent operations so that, for a fade-in, starting with no exposure and extending for a predetermined number of frames, each successive frame receives a progressively greater exposure than the frame preceding it, until full exposure for the scene is attained. From this frame on, successive frames receive identical exposure for the remainder of the take. The procedure is reversed in the case of a fade-out. (UFPA)

Fairing Calculation A planning of variable amounts of motion for starting and stopping action to give a smooth natural effect, with smaller increments plotted at the beginning and end; an "easing in" and "easing out" of motion.

Field The portion of the scene in front of the camera within the limits of the camera aperture at the focal plane. Area of field thus varies with focal length of lens, camera-to-subject distance, and size of the camera aperture. (UFPA)

Field Guide A sheet of heavy celluloid or acetate that is used for positioning artwork in relation to the camera. When the guide—upon which all of the camera fields are indicated—is placed on the registration pegs on the platen area, there is no need to view the artwork through the camera. The guide shows the exact area that will be photographed for a given lens and distance.

Field Size A measure of the size of the area being photographed on the animation stand at a given moment. Field sizes range from a 1-field to a 12-field, with the numbers referring to the width of the field in inches.

Field Step On a field guide, the individual rectangles formed by vertical and horizontal lines, or the increments between each line.

Filmograph A technique in which camera and compound movement create the illusion of motion in still pictures or artwork. Also called photographic animation.

Film Speed See **Emulsion Speed.**

Flipping A technique of viewing and roughly evaluating the smoothness of an animated sequence at the pencil drawing stage. A sheaf of drawings is usually held up with one hand and released in sequence using the thumb and index finger of the other hand.

Floating Peg Bars A set of peg bars which holds overlays or cels above the compound to create the illusion of depth. The floating peg bars function independently of the compound and its controls.

Focus (1) The point where rays of light entering a given lens, from a point on the subject, meet. (2) The degree of clarity of an image through a lens onto a screen or a film emulsion.

Footage A length of film not necessarily related to a specific number of feet; often referred to as a "take."

Foreground The part of the scene nearest to the camera.

Frame (1) A single picture in a motion picture film. (2) To bring the limits of an individual picture on a piece of motion picture film into coincidence with the limits of the projector aperture in projection (UFPA). (3) To compose a shot.

Frame Counter A digital indicator which shows the exact number of frames exposed.

Guide A pencil or ink overlay, prepared in register with the animation art, indicating the positioning of animation or camera movements.

Head On a tape recorder or projector, an electromagnet across which the tape or film is drawn and which magnetizes the coating on the tape base during recording.

Held Cel A cel that is held for several frames during some portion of an animated sequence.

Highlights Visually the brightest or photometrically the most luminant areas of a subject. In the negative image, the areas of greatest density; in the positive image, the areas of least density. (UFPA)

Hold Used to indicate a stop position for drawings or pan backgrounds when they are being photographed.

Hot Spot A part of the field that is unevenly illuminated—usually a bright area in the center.

In-between Drawings Those animation drawings between the extreme drawings, which are used to create a smooth flow of animation.

In-betweener An animator who draws the moving characters or objects between the extremes drawn by the key animator.

Inker The individual who traces the outlines from the animated drawings onto the cels.

Interlock The first synchronous presentation of the workprint and the sound track (on separate films) by means of a mechanical or an electrical link between the projector and the sound reproducer.

Key Animator The individual who draws the "key" points of movement for an animated character.

Laboratory An establishment organized and equipped to process motion picture film and to produce prerelease duplicating internegatives, such as master positives, duplicate negatives, and workprints, as well as completed release prints for distribution. (UFA)

Layout The arrangement or design of a scene. Background and characters or objects are shown in correct relative size, colors, and cel levels. Camera movement is often indicated as a part of the layout.

Light Meter See **Exposure Meter.**

Limited Animation A technique in which only one part of a character or object moves.

Lip Synchronization The relationship of sound and picture that exists when the movements of speech are perceived to coincide with the sounds of speech. (UFPA)

Live Action Sequences of a film in which live actors or real objects instead of drawings are photographed.

Long Shot The photographing of a scene or action from a distance or a wide angle of view so that a large area of the setting appears on a frame of film, and the scene or objects appear quite small.

Magnetic Tape Usually ¼-inch plastic tape that has been coated with particles that can be magnetized. Used on tape recorders as the recording medium and provides the highest fidelity of reproduction practical today. In film use, it also comes in various formats to coincide with super 8, 16 mm, and 35 mm films, and it is sprocketed.

Magnetic Track A film or tape that has been coated with a magnetic recording medium on which audio signals are recorded as variations in magnetism.

Mask A device used to block or limit the passage of light from one area while admitting whole or reduced illumination to another area. (UFPA)

Master The final or intermediate film from which subsequent prints are made.

Match-line An indication on the layout and background of where a character is cut off by the foreground. For example, an animated character driving a car could be cut off by a window in the foreground; a match-line would be drawn on the edge of the artwork to indicate this point.

Matte A dull or nonshiny surface.

Medium Shot A scene that is photographed from a medium distance so that the full figure of the subject fills an entire frame.

Mil 1/1000 of an inch. Tape thickness is usually measured in mils.

Mix The combination of various sound tracks into a single track.

Mixer The sound engineer at the mixing console who does the mixing process. Also an electronic instrument that takes in various volume-controlled signals that are fed into a single channel to form the mixed track.

Model Sheet A sheet illustrating the various sides and proportions of a character used for reference by the animation staff. There can be several model sheets to show expression as well as proportion and other details of the character.

Monitor Head The head on a tape recorder or camera that, when connected to the proper circuitry, makes it possible to listen to the material directly off the tape or film while the recording is being made.

Multiplane Developed at the Disney Studios, an animation stand with several layers of plate glass that hold cels and overlays to be filmed to create the illusion of depth.

Narration The commentary for a film spoken by an off-screen voice in "voice-over" situations.

Negative The term "negative" is used to designate any of the following (in either black-and-white or color): (1) The raw stock specifically designed for negative images. (2) The negative image. (3) Negative raw stock that has been exposed but has not been processed. (4) Processed film bearing a negative image.

Negative Image A photographic image in which the values of light and shade of the original photographed subject are represented in inverse order—light objects of the original subject are represented by high densities and dark objects are represented by low densities. In color negatives, the colors are complementary to those in the subject.

Ones, Twos, or Threes The number of frames that a cel is to be held during photography.

Opaquing Filling in the tones and colors between previously inked lines on the cels.

Optical Effects Any alteration of a motion picture scene, or transition from one scene to another, commonly introduced in duplication. Includes fades, dissolves, and wipes, as well as many more spectacular effects. (UFPA)

Original An initial photographic image, or sound recording—whether photographic, or magnetic, as opposed to some stage of duplication, thereof. (UFPA)

Overlay Usually a part of the animation cel or prop that goes over the background or object when the scene is being photographed. It is used to create the illusion of greater depth in a scene.

Pan (1) Animation: The horizontal or vertical movement of the animation compound bearing the animation artwork, while being photographed. (2) Live-Action: A horizontal scanning movement by the camera, usually from the pivotal point of a tripod.

Pan Chart A chart that is taped to the top of a cel or background that indicates a fairing calculation showing the increments of motion from start to finish.

Pantograph Unit A flat surface with a field guide mounted on it and a pointer suspended over it. Each movement of the compound is accompanied by an equivalent move of the pantograph needle over the pantograph field guide.

Parallax The apparent displacement of an object in relation to its background due to observation of the object from more than one point in space. In camera work, the viewfinder often is mounted with its optical axis at an appreciable distance from the optical axis of the camera lens, commonly resulting in inadvertent positional errors in framing.

Path of Action In the full animation of a character, the direction and amount of space to be taken by the character's motion in the field to be filmed.

Peg Bars Two sets of pegs mounted on separate mobile tracks embedded in the surface of the animation table. Artwork, with corresponding holes, is placed over the pegs to accurately align and position it on the animation stand.

Pencil Test A test in which pencil drawings or layouts are photographed instead of the finished cels in order to determine timing and corrections needed before the scene is inked and opaqued as finished art. Also called line test.

Persistence of Vision A time-lag effect between visual stimulation of the eye and cessation of response to that stimulation. For any intermittently illuminated source there is a critical frequency (which depends upon the brightness of the source) above which the average eye can detect no sensation of flicker. (UFPA)

Picture Workprint A positive print that usually consists of intercut picture daily prints, picture library prints, prints of dissolves, montages, titles, etc, and has synchronism constantly maintained with the corresponding sound workprint. A picture workprint is used as a guide by the editor in combining the various picture scenes of a motion picture into the desired form.

Pixilation A technique of shooting live action at various speeds from single-frame to half speed (12 frames a second) that shows living things moving like animated objects.

Platen A flat piece of optically clear glass that is used to hold cels in position over a background during animation photography.

Plot The calibration of camera movements prior to panning or zooming from one field guide position to another.

Positive Image A photographic replica in which the values of light and shade of the original photographed subject are represented in their natural order. The light objects of the original subject are represented by low densities and the dark objects are represented by high densities.

Post-synchronized The recording of the sound track after animation has been completed.

Presynchronized The recording of the sound track before any animation production has begun.

Production The general term used to describe the processes involved in making all the original material that is the basis for the finished motion picture. Loosely, the completed film.

Rackover A method of viewfinding and focusing in which the body of the camera is shifted to one side behind the taking lens so that the film aperture is replaced by a ground glass; the camera is shifted back to the original position before an exposure is made.

Raw Stock Motion picture film that has not been exposed or processed.

Reduction Printing The process of producing and recording photographically a smaller image—usually on a smaller film—from a larger image. Film thus made is referred to as a reduction negative or a reduction print, whichever is applicable. Example: a super 8 print can be made from a 16 mm original, or a 16 mm print can be made from 35 mm.

Registration (1) The positioning of a drawing, cel, or background on the pegs of an animation board so that all work is aligned. (1) The precise locating in the camera of each frame of film.

Release Print A composite print made for general distribution and exhibition after the final trial composite or answer print has been approved.

Reversal Film A film which, after exposure, is processed to produce a positive image on the same film rather than a negative image. (If exposure is made by printing from a negative, a reversal stock will yield another negative.)

Reverse Cycling The procedure of shooting the same scene forward and backward (for example, moving a valve up and then down).

Rotoscope A device (developed by the Fleischer studios) that is used to project live-action images on a screen where they are then traced by an animator to capture a difficult life movement or to economize on time. Also used to make layouts, traveling mattes, and silhouette images in animation.

Rushes See **Dailies.**

Scene (1) A continuously developed unit of action in a film. (2) A shot.

Scratch-off A process wherein portions of inked and opaqued cels are either scratched off or erased during photography; often shot with the camera operating in reverse, so the material appears to grow into finished form rather than disappear.

Self Line An ink or electrostatic line on the cel which is the same color as the subject instead of the customary black line.

Sequence A series of shots characterized by unity of theme and purpose; (UFPA) see (2) below.

Shot (1) A single run of the camera. (2) The piece of film resulting from such a run. Systematically joined together in the process of editing, shots are synthesized first into scenes; the scenes are joined to form sequences, and the sequences, in turn, are joined to form the film as a whole. (UFPA)

Shutter In a motion picture camera, the mechanical device that shields the film from light at the aperture during the film-movement portion of the intermittent cycle. Also, a similar device in projectors for cutting the projection light during the time the film is moving at the aperture. (UFPA)

Single-frame Exposure The exposure of one frame of motion picture film at a time, in the manner of still photography. Commonly used in animation because of the need to make changes of cels or in the relationship of the compound to the camera.

Slide/Motion Film See **Filmograph.**

Sliding Cels Longer-than-standard-size cels. Used for panning and special effects.

Sound Effects Any sound from any source other than the tracks bearing synchronized dialogue, narration, or music; sound effects are commonly introduced into a master track in the rerecording step, usually with the idea of enhancing the illusion of reality in the finished presentation. (UFPA)

Sound-on-sound A method in which previously recorded material on one track may be rerecorded on another track while simultaneously adding new material (sound). Sound added to a previous recording may be called sound-on-sound, but has disadvantages, and is not a professional way to add, for example, background music to a sound recording.

Sound Reader A device used for playback of sound tracks, particularly during the editing procedure. (UFPA)

Sound Track The portion of a length of film reserved for the sound record. Also, any length of film bearing sound only. (UFPA)

Special Effects Any shot unobtainable by straightforward motion picture shooting techniques.

Splicer A mechanical device that holds two pieces of film or tape in alignment (with the correct sprocket hole interval for film) while they are joined together with cement, tape, ultrasonics, etc.

Splicing Tape A special pressure-sensitive nonmagnetic tape used for splicing magnetic recording tape or a similar tape used for splicing film.

Squash and Stretch In full animation, the exaggerated rendering of a moving object to emphasize and enhance the illusion of motion and increase its vitality.

Stop The relationship between the focal length of a lens and the effective diameter of its aperture. An adjustable iris diaphragm permits any ordinary photographic lens to be used at any stop within its range.

Stop Down To decrease the diameter of the light-admitting orifice of a lens by adjustment of an iris diaphragm. (UFPA)

Storyboard A pictorial outline of a film presentation, based on sketches of representative situations, and designed to accompany a draft of a script as an aid in visualizing the ideas involved.

Strobing Uncontrolled series of short, staccato jumping movements on the screen, caused by faulty animation technique, camera work, or equipment; also called jitter.

Synchronization The positioning of a sound track so that it is exactly timed to the picture portion of the film.

Synchronizer A mechanism employing a common rotary shaft that has sprockets which, by engaging perforations in the film, pass identical lengths of picture and sound films simultaneously, thus keeping the two (or more) films in synchronization during the editing process. (UFPA) Often referred to as a "gang synchronizer," indicating multiple sprockets.

Tabletop See **Compound.**

Take A term used to indicate the number of times a given shot has been made. Takes are usually numbered sequentially and identified in the picture by slate and in the track by voice. (UFPA)

Title The name or designation of a film. Also, any inscription contained in a film for the purpose of conveying information about the film, its message, or its story to the viewer. (UFPA)

Top Pegs The upper set of pegs on an animation board or camera compound table, used for registering drawings, cels, or backgrounds.

Transition The passage from one episodic part to another. Usually, film transitions are accomplished rapidly and smoothly, without loss of audience orientation, and are consistent with the established mood of the film. (UFPA)

Traveling Matte 1. A matte film which travels through a printer with the printing film to create a certain effect. (UFA). 2. Involves a technique for combining two or more separate images, moving in relation to each other, on a finished motion picture film so that each image occupies a portion of each frame without overlapping the other image. Commonly used to combine live action and animation.

Traveling Pegs The registration pegs on the compound, which can be moved by bars set in the compound table. Used for panning purposes.

Trucking To move a camera translationally in space as a shot proceeds, usually by means of a dolly or other vehicular camera support. The purpose is to pace and maintain image size of moving subjects.

Twos See **Ones, Twos, or Threes.**

Viewer A mechanical and optical device designed to permit examination of an enlarged image of motion picture film. (UFA)

Viewfinder A camera component arranged to indicate the boundaries of the camera's field of view.

Voice-over A sound and picture relationship in which an off-screen narrator's voice accompanies picture action. (UFA)

Wipe An optical effect used as a transition from one scene to another. In its commonest form, scene "A" appears to be "wiped" off the screen by the progressive revelation of scene "B" as a vertical dividing line separating the two advances across the screen usually from left to right. (UFPA)

Workprint Any picture or sound track print, usually a positive, intended for use in the editing process to establish through a series of trial cuttings the finished version of a film. The purpose is to preserve the original intact (and undamaged) until the final cutting points have been established. (UFPA)

Zoom In A continuous approach by the camera to the subject, which gradually narrows down the area of the picture being photographed, giving the effect of continuously enlarging the subject.

Zoom Lens A lens whose focal length is variable within specified limits, and is capable of simulating the effect of the camera's movement toward or away from a subject.

Zoom Out A progressive retreat from the subject, which gradually enlarges the area being photographed, giving the effect of a continuously diminishing subject.

PART TWELVE

Sources of Animation Equipment and Materials

Courtesy of Cartoon Colour, Inc.

EQUIPMENT

ARRIFLEX CORPORATION
1 Westchester Plaza
Elmsford, N.Y. 10523

BIRNS AND SAWYER, INC.
1026 North Highland Ave.
Hollywood, Calif. 90038

CAMERA MART, INC.
456 West 55th St.
New York, N.Y. 10019

CARTOON COLOUR, INC.
9024 Lindblade St.
Culver City, Calif. 90230

VICTOR DUNCAN, INC.
200 East Ontario
Chicago, Ill. 60611

2659 Fondren
Dallas, Tex. 75206

32380 Howard
Madison Heights, Mich. 48071

FAX COMPANY
374 South Fair Oaks Ave.
Pasadena, Calif. 91105

F&B CECO/S.O.S.
315 West 43rd St.
New York, N.Y. 10036

7051 Santa Monica Blvd.
Los Angeles, Calif. 90038

FOROX CORPORATION
511 Center Ave.
Mamaroneck, N.Y. 10543

ALAN GORDON ENTERPRISES, INC.
1430 North Cahuenga Blvd.
Hollywood, Calif. 90028

LYON LAMB
Video Animation System
2132 Benecia Ave.
Los Angeles, Calif. 90025

OXBERRY
Division of Richmark Camera Service
180 Broad St.
Carlstadt, N.J. 07072

OX PRODUCTS, INC.
180 East Prospect Ave.
Mamaroneck, N.Y. 10543

STORYBOARDS, PLANNING BOARDS, AND PLANNING CARDS

MEDRO EDUCATIONAL PRODUCTS
P.O. Box 8463
Rochester, N.Y. 14618

DIMENSIONAL LETTERS

HERNARD MFG. CO., INC.
375 Executive Blvd.
Elmsford, N.Y. 10523

MITTEN DESIGNER LETTERS
85 Fifth Ave.
New York, N.Y. 10003

LETTERING SYSTEMS

Chartpak:
CHARTPAK
1 River Rd.
Leeds, Mass. 01053

Geotype:
DEANS GEOGRAPHICS, LTD.
1110 Seymour St.
Vancouver, B.C., V6B 3N3,
Canada

Leroy Lettering Set:
KEUFFEL & ESSER CO.
40 East 43rd St.
New York, N.Y. 10017

Leteron:
REYNOLDS/LETERON
13425 Wyandotte St.
North Hollywood, Calif. 91605

Letraset Instant Lettering:
LETRASET U.S.A., INC.
40 Eisenhower Dr.
Paramus, N.J. 07652

Letterguide:
LETTERGUIDE, INC.
P.O. Box 30203
Lincoln, Nebr. 68503

Normatype:
KEUFFEL & ESSER CO.
40 East 43rd St.
New York, N.Y. 10017

Prestype:
PRESTYPE, INC.
194 Veterans Blvd.
Carlstadt, N.J. 07072

RapiDesign (templates and lettering guides):
BEROL USA
Division of Berol Corporation
Danbury, Conn. 06810

Tactype:
TACTYPE
127 West 26th St.
New York, N.Y. 10001

Varigraph:
VARIGRAPH, INC.
1480 Martin St.
P.O. Box 690
Madison, Wis. 53701

Wrico:
THE WOOD-REGAN
INSTRUMENT CO., INC.
15 Label St.
Montclair, N.J. 07042

Zipatone:
ZIPATONE, INC.
150 Fenc'l La.
Hillside, Ill. 60162

HOT-PRESS LETTERING

Tel-Anima Print, Hot Press:
S.O.S. PHOTO-CINE-OPTICS, INC.
315 West 43rd St.
New York, N.Y. 10036

7051 Santa Monica Blvd.
Hollywood, Calif. 90038

COLORED PAPER

Bull's Eye Art Paper:
MILTON BRADLEY CO.
Springfield, Mass. 01101

Color-Aid, Color-Vu, Tru-Tone:
LEWIS ARTISTS' MATERIALS, INC.
18 East 53rd St.
New York, N.Y. 10022

ARTHUR BROWN & BRO., INC.
2 West 46th St.
New York, N.Y. 10036

CEL SUPPLIES

CARTOON COLOUR, INC.
9024 Lindblade St.
Culver City, Calif. 90230

HEATH PRODUCTIONS, INC.
1700 North Westshore Blvd.
Tampa, Fla. 33607

CHARRETTE
31 Olympia Ave.
Woburn, Mass. 01801

WORLD SUPPLY, INC.
3425 West Cahuenga Blvd.
Hollywood, Calif. 90068

S.O.S. PHOTO-CINE-OPTICS, INC.
315 West 43rd St.
New York, N.Y. 10036

7051 Santa Monica Blvd.
Hollywood, Calif. 90038

COLOR CRAYONS, PENCILS, AND PENS

Blaisdell Paper Wrapped Pencils and Markers,
Liquid Tip Permanent Markers:
BEROL USA
Division of Berol Corporation
Danbury, Conn. 06810

Faber-Castell Pens:
PLAZA ARTISTS' MATERIALS
173 Madison Ave.
New York, N.Y. 10016

Koh-I-Noor Rapidographic Technical Drawing Pens:
KOH-I-NOOR RAPIDOGRAPH, INC.
100 North St.
Bloomsbury, N.J. 08804

Lumocolor Pens and Markers:
J. S. STAEDTLER, INC.
P.O. Box 787
Chatsworth, Calif. 91311

P.O. Box 68
Montville, N.J. 07045

STAEDTLER-MARS LTD.
6 Mars Rd.
Rexdale, Ontario, M9V 2K1,
Canada

Mars Technical Pens:
J. S. STAEDTLER, INC.
P.O. Box 787
Chatsworth, Calif. 91311

P.O. Box 68
Montville, N.J. 07045

STAEDTLER-MARS LTD.
6 Mars Rd.
Rexdale, Ontario, M9V 2K1,
Canada

Prismacolor Art Markers and Art Pencils:
BEROL, USA
Division of Berol Corporation
Danbury, Conn. 06810

INKS AND PAINTS

ARTHUR BROWN & BRO., INC.
2 West 46th St.
New York, N.Y. 10036

CARTOON COLOUR CO., INC.
9024 Lindblade St.
Culver City, Calif. 90230

Grumbacher Designer's Colors:
ARTHUR BROWN & BRO., INC.
2 West 46th St.
New York, N.Y. 10036

Dr. P. H. Martin's Dyes:
SALIS INTERNATIONAL
4040 North 29th Ave.
Hollywood, Fla. 33020

PLAZA ARTISTS' MATERIALS
173 Madison Ave.
New York, N.Y. 10016

EXPOSURE SHEETS

S.O.S. PHOTO-CINE-OPTICS, INC.
315 West 43rd St.
New York, N.Y. 10036

7051 Santa Monica Blvd.
Hollywood, Calif. 90038

CARTOON COLOUR, INC.
9024 Lindblade St.
Culver City, Calif. 90230

REGISTRATION DEVICES

S.O.S. PHOTO-CINE-OPTICS, INC.
315 West 43rd St.
New York, N.Y. 10036

7051 Santa Monica Blvd.
Hollywood, Calif. 90038

OXBERRY
Division of Richmark Camera Service
180 Broad St.
Carlstadt, N.J. 07072

FIELD GUIDES

OXBERRY
Division of Richmark Camera Service
180 Broad St.
Carlstadt, N.J. 07072

S.O.S. PHOTO-CINE-OPTICS, INC.
315 West 43rd St.
New York, N.Y. 10036

7051 Santa Monica Blvd.
Hollywood, Calif. 90036

CARTOON COLOUR, INC.
9024 Lindblade St.
Culver City, Calif. 90230

MISCELLANEOUS SUPPLIES

CARTOON COLOUR, INC.
9024 Lindblade St.
Culver City, Calif. 90230

Inquiries should be sent to the above suppliers. Inclusion of a firm in this listing does not imply preference, endorsement, or recommendation by Eastman Kodak Company.

BIBLIOGRAPHY

Anderson, Joseph and Barbara Fisher, JOURNAL OF THE UNIVERSITY FILM ASSOCIATION, "The Myth of Persistence of Vision." University Film Association, 1978, Vol. XXX No. 4

Blair, Preston, ANIMATION, Walter T. Foster, 1949

Cabarga, Leslie, THE FLEISCHER STORY, New York: Nostalgia Press, Franklin Square, 1976

Canemaker, John, THE ANIMATED RAGGEDY ANN & ANDY, New York: Bobbs-Merrill, 1977

Edera, Bruno, FULL LENGTH ANIMATED FEATURE FILMS, New York: Hastings House, 1977

FACTFILE #9, The American Film Institute, November 1977

Finch, Christopher, THE ART OF WALT DISNEY, New York: Harry N. Abrams, Inc., 1973

Fitzsimmons, John A., "My Days with Winsor McCay," unpublished letter, Woody Gelman collection, New York: Nostalgia Press, Franklin Square

Halas, John, Roger Manwell, THE TECHNIQUE OF ANIMATION, New York: Hastings House, 1968

Heath, Robert, ANIMATION IN 12 HARD LESSONS, Heath Productions, 1972

Horn, Maurice, THE WORLD ENCYCLOPEDIA OF COMICS, New York: Chelsea House Publishers, 1976

London, Mel, GETTING INTO FILM, New York: Ballantine Books, 1977

Madsen, Roy P., ANIMATED FILM, New York: Interland Publishing, 1969

Maltin, Leonard, THE DISNEY FILMS, New York: Crown, 1973

Perisic, Zoran, THE ANIMATION STAND, New York: Hastings House, Focal Press Limited, 1976

Robinson, Jerry, THE COMICS, The Newspaper Comics Council, New York: Berkley Publishing Corporation, 1974

Russett, Robert and Cecile Starr, EXPERIMENTAL ANIMATION, New York: Van Nostrand Reinhold Company, Litton Educational Publishing, Inc., 1976

Thomas, Robert, THE ART OF ANIMATION, New York: Golden Press, 1958, Walt Disney Productions

Thomas, Robert, WALT DISNEY—AN AMERICAN ORIGINAL, New York: Simon and Shuster, 1976

Salt, Brian, BASIC ANIMATION STAND TECHNIQUES, Oxford: Pergamon Press, 1977

Smith, Conrad, JOURNAL OF THE UNIVERSITY FILM ASSOCIATION, University Film Association, 1977, Vol. XXIX No. 3

TIME Magazine, MILESTONES COLUMN, September 25, 1972

Author unlisted, ANIMATED CARTOONS FOR THE BEGINNER, Walter T. Foster, date & copyright unlisted

Additional information from

Computer Image Corporation, Denver, CO
Walt Disney Productions, Burbank, CA
DePatie-Freleng Enterprises, Inc., Friz Freleng, Van Nuys, CA
Cartoon Colour Co. Inc., Culver City, CA
Filmation Studios, Reseda, CA
Oxberry, Carlstadt, NJ
Raoul Servais, Brussels
Hanna-Barbera Productions, Hollywood
Richard Williams Animation Studio London, Hollywood
Chuck Jones, Hollywood
Bob Kurtz & Friends, Hollywood
Warner Brothers, Burbank, CA
Maxwell Seligman, Tele-Craft, New York
Phil Kimmelman, New York
John Canemaker, New York
Francis Lee, Film Planning Associates, New York
Al Stahl Animated, New York

INDEX

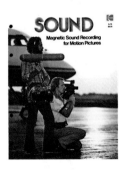

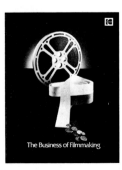

KODAK PUBLICATIONS

Eastman Kodak Company's Motion Picture and Audiovisual Markets Division also produces a wide selection of data books addressing many different filmmaking topics. Described below are some of the Kodak publications that we think will be of particular interest to those of you working or planning to work in the field of motion picture production.

P-18

Basic Production Techniques for Motion Pictures, $3 This Data Book is intended to assist individuals and groups in business, education, government, industry, medicine, etc, in making effective motion picture films. It is directed primarily to the beginning producer of small-scale, in-plant motion pictures and covers planning, equipment, films, lighting, editing, titling, sound, filmmaking language, special applications, etc.

H-1

Selection and Use of KODAK and EASTMAN Motion Picture Films, $3 This Data Book is intended to help those engaged in motion picture film production choose the film or films best suited to their particular application and obtain the best results from the stocks selected. Subjects covered include emulsion characteristics, filters, printing, processing, sound, physical characteristics, packaging, film care and storage, and industry standards. Price includes choice of current film data sheets.

S-75

SOUND: Magnetic Sound Recording for Motion Pictures, $6.25 This Data Book illustrates the vital role played by the sound track of any motion picture and will familiarize the reader with today's techniques in achieving top-quality sound reproduction.

H-2

Cinematographer's Field Guide—Motion Picture Camera Films, $3.95 This handy, pocket-size publication is our new "bible" for anyone interested in KODAK and EASTMAN Professional Motion Picture Camera Films. Designed to withstand heavy day-to-day use, the H-2 Guide will go on assignment with you any time, any place, and always be available to help you choose and order the right camera film for your needs. It is divided into five major sections including film and filter data, usage hints, film packaging, and ordering.

S-12

IMAGES, IMAGES, IMAGES—The Book of Programmed Multi-Image Production. $15.95. This comprehensive book details the planning, producing, and presenting of multi-image (multiprojector) shows. It examines the reasons why multi-image is so strikingly successful as a communications medium and the many elements that contribute to informative, inspiring presentations. Some of the major subjects include determining your visual style, researching before writing the script, shooting your slides, and much more. And you'll find information on creating animation with slides in this exciting medium.

H-55

The Business of Filmmaking—$6.95 This Data Book details the business side of planning, producing, and distributing successful nontheatrical motion picture films. The content stresses efficient use of management and selling skills in filmmaking. Some of the major topics covered are planning sales calls, determining client needs, preparing and presenting the film proposal, securing the production contract, controlling production costs, choosing postproduction options, promoting and distributing the film, and managing your finances.

Literature Packets

For your future convenience, the publications described to the left, this book (S-35), and a variety of appropriate catalogs and resource listings have been gathered together as the BASIC FILMMAKER'S PACKET, Kodak Publication No. H-100 ($28.50). Taken as a whole, the packet provides many practical and up-to-date insights into the fascinating realm of professional filmmaking—information that will help you satisfy both today's AND tomorrow's challenging communication needs.

Another equally comprehensive packet covering a different area of film application is the FILM IN TELEVISION PACKET, Kodak Publication No. H-200 ($9.00). This packet provides broad coverage on the many uses of still and motion picture films in the television environment.

Ordering Information

See the reply form attached at the back of this book for details on ordering these publications.

For a complete listing of all Kodak motion picture and audiovisual publications, fill in the information requested on the publications index coupon, fold up the form, and drop it in the mail for one free copy of MP&AVMD PUBLICATIONS INDEX (S-4).